# THE F WORD

# THE F WORD

## HOW TO SURVIVE YOUR FAMILY

# Louie Anderson

### with CARL KURLANDER

**WARNER BOOKS**

An AOL Time Warner Company

An AOL Time Warner Company

Printed in the United States of America

ISBN: 0-446-53017-4

*Book design and text composition by L&G McRee*

# Author's Note

In this book, the identities of certain family members, friends, and acquaintances have been obscured or their names changed.

I have great affection for those who've been kind enough to share family stories and lessons learned. To them, I owe my deepest gratitude.

—LOUIE ANDERSON, May 2002

# Acknowledgments

To my family for once again allowing me to share their lives with strangers. I realized in writing this book how we are all in the same boat on this journey, and I appreciate the good company.

To my friends, those who have become a part of my new extended family in many ways. It would take another book just to list you all here, but I have learned from you the possibilities of what families can be. Though we may float in and out of each other's lives, you are always in my heart.

To the people who helped directly bring this book into existence, this has been such a personal experience for me; I hope you have gotten out of this even a small part of how much you have given of yourselves in making this a reality. My greatest thanks to David Vigliano, a super agent and a funny guy in his own right. To Rick Horgan, an editor who pushed us to help this book reach its potential even when we at times resisted; to the other good folks at Warner Books: Jackie Meyer, Christine Dao, Madeleine Schachter, Katharine Rapkin, Bob Castillo, Jim Spivey, Tom Whatley, Heidi Winter, and H. B. Fenn. To Alex Murray for encouraging me to do this book in the first place. To Scott Hunter for working so diligently on getting together everything we needed. To Aaron Schlichting for working so hard on the original illustrations. To Dave Gilbertson for reading the drafts, giving us feedback, and introducing us to your wonderful family from North Dakota. To Jim Gitar, who has often been there for me as a father, a brother, a golfing buddy, a manager, and a friend. To Mildred Newman, who helped us and would have loved this book. To Natalie Kurlander for putting up with my borrowing her husband for so long (although at times I'm sure it was a blessing); and to Campbell Kurlander—the world's smartest three-year-old—for letting her Daddy spend time with me he would have been spending reading you a story. To Carl Kurlander, who has been my friend for fifteen years and, in some ways, my twelfth sibling: This book has taught us both what collaboration means—and is in many ways a product of our long-running, continual dialogue. And don't think it has stopped just because the book is over. To Abraham Geisness, for being my spiritual guide, my good friend, and a person who is not afraid to always tell the truth.

And finally, to my fans, who have been there with me through all these years. You are the family I am so lucky to have. The ones who bring me the unconditional love I wish for each of you. Your support means so much. I'll see you at the shows, but please feel free to let me know your thoughts about this book by e-mailing me at www.louieanderson.com.

No matter how hard I try, no matter how much money I spend, no matter how much I *pray*, there's no way I can change, fix, or reinvent my family. But still I try.

July – 1943

# Contents

# The F Word

Survey says . . . family. In a recent survey, when people were asked what they wanted most, they didn't answer: wealth, fame, or to golf better than Tiger Woods. Instead, the number one answer was "to resolve some problem with my family."

Let's be honest, folks. Some of us have a better chance of defeating Tiger Woods at the Masters than fixing our families. Some of us may even think we'd be better off using a golf club on our families to resolve problems. In golf, we can at least learn a stance, a grip, a swing. But there's no instructional guide for dealing with our loved—or *not* so loved—ones.

All of us have memories of Dad kneeling on the floor Christmas morning, instructions laid out, trying to put together a bike or wagon. In the Anderson house, we were lucky if my father even glanced at those instructions (if he did, it was only after the surrender of his know-it-all attitude). As he'd proudly present me with his version of a two-wheel Schwinn glider, I'd notice some extra pieces lying on the floor. "Hey, Dad, what are these for?" He'd glare at me. As he grabbed the bolts and tossed them in the drawer, he'd explain, "They only throw in those things so they can jack up the price."

Even if there *were* an instruction book on how to raise a family, my dad probably wouldn't have read it. The only thing I know for sure—after experiencing two parents, four grandparents, ten brothers and sisters, twenty-seven nieces and nephews, and over twenty great-nieces and nephews—is that there's not *one* set of instructions for making families function. That's why I've decided to share my forty-nine years of family experiences and some ideas that worked and some that didn't.

When I wrote my first book, *Dear Dad,* I was trying to make peace with my deceased father whose alcoholism had damaged everyone in my family. This book is more about finding peace with those he left behind, those whom I care about most but who often—unintentionally—cause me the most pain. (I'm sure I cause *them* pain as well.) In this era in which dysfunctional families are more the norm than the exception, a survival guide might help a lot of us. I don't think I'm alone in trying to deal with family squabbles, family reunions, family finances, and family histories. (Maybe you're getting a sense of why I titled this book *The F Word.*) My hope is that what I'll be saying here will inspire people and help them understand that we're all trying to get to the same destination.

I realize that many of *my* experiences are darker than most. A lot of people come from wonderful, happy homes. Their success stories just don't get the press. You never see an anchor from *Dateline* announce, "Tonight the Smiths had a nice family dinner, enjoyed a movie together, and kissed each other goodnight." Doing comedy around the country, I've met many great families and have learned a lot from them. Much of their wisdom is included in what follows. But even these great families acknowledge there's always room for improvement. When I was hosting *Family Feud*, I ended each showing by telling audiences "Be good to your families." This book tries to show how.

# THE F WORD

# Fatal Mistake

## (almost)

I'm in Vegas in the house where I've come to live for a year, escaping Los Angeles. It's not lost on me that this is where Nick Cage's character in *Leaving Las Vegas* comes after being sick of L.A., and when he is drinking too much. Ultimately, the movie makes clear that, for the Cage character, "leaving Las Vegas" means never leaving at all.

It's a Thursday and I'm about to start a two-week stint headlining at Bally's casino. I don't think I can get through it. Even if I do, the money I make will just go to pay government back taxes. I've pissed away so much money—by purchasing crap, hiring too many employees, and gambling—that I'm now $500,000 in debt. If that's not enough, I'm being blackmailed by someone who's threatening to undermine my career. The world seems like a cruel place.

I own a .38-caliber nickel-plated Smith and Wesson that on this particular day is loaded. I used to do a routine in my act about how I came to buy the gun in Wyoming when I was shooting a movie. I bought it just because it was easy to buy a gun in Wyoming. I'd never even thought about getting one, but was intrigued by the idea of owning a gun just like James Bond's. When the gun turned out to be the same price as what the filmmakers were paying me as a daily allowance, I bought it. Complete with matching bullets.

But this is no routine. I'm holding the gun in my hand. No one is home and I turn the TV to a music station and crank it up loud so the gun's sound will be muffled. I sit next to the blaring speakers and pray for a reason to continue with my screwed-up life. I search for something positive, *anything*. The "poor me" part of myself has a firm hold and isn't willing to let go.

I cock the gun, pull back the trigger, and rather than see my life flashing before me, I remember something I once saw on a TV special. It was a law enforcement person saying that, contrary to movie depictions of someone putting a gun to his head and efficiently ending his life, many times the person will survive but end up paralyzed or brain damaged. The expert helpfully pointed out where one should place a gun to achieve certain death. With the weapon all set, I say my prayers and ask for forgiveness for what I'm about to do.

Except I must first wait for a good, loud heavy-metal song. You don't want to die on a bad song. Back when I drove a lot to gigs, I used to think how terrible it would be to die in a car accident with some annoying song on

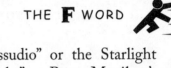

the radio. Phil Collins's "Sussudio" or the Starlight Vocal Band's "Afternoon Delight" or Barry Manilow's "Looks Like We Made It." You don't want any of *those* to be the last thing you hear in life.

I sit against the wall and have a strange thought about the mess this is going to make. (My mother raised me well.) So I get up and fetch a towel to drape over my head. Finally, I'm all set and I cock the gun again, place it in the right spot, put my heavy thumb on the trigger and almost on cue, the right song comes on. Just as I put pressure on the trigger, the song volume lowers for a chorus and I have time to think about who'll find me dead. A couple people come to mind. *This will really hurt them,* I think. But I'm too full of sadness and self-pity. I never wanted to hurt anyone, but I *have* to do this. Am I a coward or what?

At that moment, there's a knock at my door. *Damn . . .* my assistant and manager have been out playing golf. I yell out "Who is it?" throw the towel off, and uncock the gun, slipping it under my pillow. Unlocking the door, I discover my longtime friend and manager Jim.

"Hey, Lou, it's almost time for the show. You ready?"

"Yeah, I lost track of time. I'll be right out."

I guess even when you're about to off yourself, the show must go on. Looking back on it, there's nothing more surreal than the feeling of doing comedy minutes after you're sure you're going to be dead.

Before I walk out on stage, I say a little prayer: *God, please give me a sign that you want me to stay on this earth. Do it during this show, otherwise I see no reason why afterward I shouldn't finish what I started.*

The crowd for this performance is great and all is going well comedy-wise when suddenly I'm no longer in

my body, but am looking at myself performing. I can't
hear anything, but I can see myself doing my act. And
when I look out at the audience they're laughing and
having a good time. As soon as I notice this, their move-
ments slow to a crawl, as if I'm watching the scene in
slow motion. They rock back and forth, laughing hard.
Then, all at once, I'm back, not sure what just happened.
I smile to myself and thank God. I've had my sign.

You see, when I saw those people laughing in slow
motion, I knew that, for those few minutes, they were
free of anything and everything that was bothering
them. And I knew that not only my purpose but my *gift*
was to continue doing comedy as long as I could.

In some ways, the audience has become my family—
the perfect family we can all live with. They come for an
hour, laugh at everything I say, give me money and love,
applaud and go home. Of course, that's a fantasy family.
And though the love of an audience is real, I know that
at the end of the day I still have to deal with my real
family.

You didn't really think I was going to kill myself, did
you? Of course not—I wrote this book. We *all* have dark
times. How well we cope with them is a measure of who
we are and how well we've come to accept things. Sometimes I wonder if suicide is a failure of family. Don't
misunderstand me, I'm not saying that a victim's family
has necessarily done something wrong. But to take your
own life, you have to feel very little connection to the
world. You wonder why people in their bleakest
moments don't reach out to their families. Maybe
because they've learned that their loved ones can't
handle the truth about what went on in their lives. Or
maybe they're so mad at their relatives they're not going

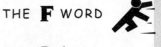

to share themselves and get hurt again. Perhaps somewhere down the line, they were taught hopelessness. I've heard stories about families where the parents killed themselves and, years later, one of the kids did too. Maybe that was their way of connecting to their parents.

Whatever suicide's underlying factors are, I didn't go through with it. Maybe in some subtle way that I didn't recognize at the time I was taught that we Andersons are survivors.

I realize that most people don't have such a desperate reaction to their families. But many people—even from good, stable homes—sometimes have dark thoughts that surprise even them. A few years have passed since the Las Vegas incident and I'm in a much different place now. It's taken me a long time to accept myself and my family. I've learned there are no simple solutions.

Not that I'm lovey-dovey with them all the time. But the Vegas close call put me on a new path. It made me want to come to terms with who I am and where I come from, and to be okay with that. And that journey inevitably leads back to family. Somewhere deep down I knew that if I were to save myself, I needed to make peace with the people I grew up with, and the events we all experienced.

# Forty-nine Family Survival Tips

Why forty-nine? Because I'm forty-nine years old and I figure, when you average it out, people learn one important truth, belief, or fact about their family a year. Of course, that's an average. Some years you might learn four; other years, nothing. Throughout the book, I'll share some of my family experiences: mistakes I've made, moments I would have handled differently, tactics that actually helped. I'm calling them "tips," but some are simply observations—ones I hope will be helpful in not only coping with, but understanding your family.

Let's face it—every family is different, every situation unique. Sometimes I've followed my own advice and felt brilliant; other times, I've asked myself, "What was I thinking?" My "process," if you can call it that, tends to work like this: "Why can't I get along with my family better? Why can't I? Why can't I? No, that's not it. Wait, here it is. No, that isn't it." It's sort of a "make it up as you go along" approach.

But I *have* learned a tremendous amount from the families I've met on the road. They apparently connect with what I'm saying, and they feel compelled to share stories—of a dad who was never there, of a grandfather who beat them, of a son who was a heroin addict. Looking at these people, I never would have guessed. Often, I realize that, even though I'm paid nicely and receive a certain amount of fame for my work, the true compensation is this wealth of personal stories people have shared with me. Many of the tips I'll be passing along derive from these tales.

## FAMILY SURVIVAL TIPS

### (a few to start off with)

**#1 Don't blame your parents because they didn't read the instructions.** Remember: for them, there was no manual either. Parents "learn on the job."

**#2 It's never too early to say "I love you."** When 9/11 happened, people immediately reached out to the ones they were close to. The first thing most of us thought was *Oh my gosh, what about the families of all those victims?* Sadly, it sometimes takes a shock like that to get us to realize what's important. We don't have to wait for a national tragedy to make that phone call we really should make. Make it *now*.

During my stand-up show in Vegas, I always encourage people to work to eliminate whatever friction they may have with their family. Once Evil Knievel came backstage and told me that, after seeing one of my previous shows, he'd gotten back in touch with his son Robbie. If a guy who has the courage to jump over the Snake River Canyon on a motorcycle fears reaching out to his kid, then clearly, healing old wounds isn't easy for anyone. But we have to make the attempt.

**#3 Your family starts with you.** In dealing with family, first you have to deal with yourself. There was a time when I didn't want to deal with anything. As often happens, that turned out to be the beginning of the journey.

**#4 Sometimes you have to ask God, or whomever, for a sign.** These days, it's easy not to believe in something. We live in cynical times where more time is spent thinking about getting a satellite dish than getting a sign from above. Even though organized religion isn't my cup of tea, I believe it's good to try to reach out to whatever Almighty we believe in whenever we can. I have a friend who does his meditation every morning on the treadmill. I sometimes say my prayers driving. (And so do some of the passengers who've seen me drive.) But it's important to remember that we're part of something greater than ourselves. Otherwise, we may be lost.

**#5 Family flu.** Feeling bad can be good. It is your heart's way of telling you that something is wrong. It's similar to that sputter your car makes. When it occurs, you know it's time to take that wreck into the shop. *Listen* to your sadness and know that in the end truth is the ultimate antidote. Depression is you telling yourself you have to change.

**#6 You always have family . . . or . . . your family always has you.** Many people could get washed up on an uninhabited island with no phone or other ways to communicate, and still, their thoughts and actions would have their basis in how they relate to their family.

# Family Matrix

*Mirror, mirror on the wall, have I become my parents once and for all?*

Like it or not, it's become apparent that many of my daily actions, rituals, and tics are either inherited or the result of early indoctrination. For example, I often like being in my bed. In fact, I'm in my bed as I write this, but only recently have I realized why. I'll often invite people into my bedroom where we talk, watch TV, or even eat. While growing up, my dad's drinking tirades often took place in the living room or the kitchen, so when my mom was fed up she'd retreat to her bedroom. Often, my siblings and I would join her there to talk softly or watch TV. So I wonder if I stay in my room now to feel safer or closer to my mom?

In reflecting on how many of my rituals or daily routines have been passed down from my parents, I can't help thinking of the movie *The Matrix*. In the film Keanu Reeves believes he's living a normal life. But then, like Alice falling down the rabbit hole, he gets sucked into an alternate reality. Eventually, Keanu's character comes to realize that the life he's living isn't real. It's an illusion. In fact, he and everyone else who think they're living their lives are actually asleep in pods that power the energy matrix—all that's left of the planet.

What does any of this have to do with family? To me, the movie is really about being asleep in our own lives, and about going deep into our subconscious to find out what's really going on.

I believe there are family matrixes that claim all of us. Each of us thinks we're living in our own world, but we're actually living in the world of our parents. You may think it's *you* getting up at two in the morning to eat a peanut butter and banana sandwich, but it's actually your dad who used to do the same thing. Just as *The Matrix* was celebrated for its special effects, our family matrixes display their own stunning effects. Case in point: the way our parents—even after they're deceased—control our thoughts and actions. *The Matrix* dazzled with slow-action kung fu; our parents also cast a kind of spell, giving us guilt trips.

Go ahead—no matter how old you are, no matter how many miles away from home—just try to walk outside in cold weather with wet hair without hearing your mother's voice telling you to put a hat on or you'll die of pneumonia. Further proof of family matrixes' special effects is that we never see our parents as they really are. They'll always be those giants who can scare away the monsters in our closets, or save our lemonade stand by adding sugar to the lemonade to make it taste good. What illusionists!

In *The Matrix,* the bad guys plant a high-tech tracking device in Keanu's body. Using a special instrument, the rebel forces are able to suck the bug right out. Unfortunately, I've yet to locate the chip my parents have put inside me. How did they take over our brains?

Prepare yourself. I'm about to go deep into my own

family's matrix. To do that, I'm going to take a day in my life and point out how many times the matrix subtly influences my actions. I'll start with waking up, because for the most part sleeping doesn't come easy for me. I always feel cheated that I have to wake up. My dad was the same way: not a morning person. I head for the kitchen where I prepare my first cup of coffee. I like weak over-creamed coffee. Almost milk with a little coffee. I can hear my dad complaining to my mom how weak the coffee is. He called it "piss water."

As I look around the kitchen, I may start to quietly straighten things up like my mother did. Or I may throw things around like my dad. I can still hear him bellow, when he'd encounter a morning mess in the kitchen: "Jeez, can't anyone put anything away! What—does this friggin' stuff climb out of the refrigerator in the middle of the night and sit on the counter? This cheese is hard as a rock!" But when my mother or one of my sisters would start cleaning up, we'd hear him protest: "Don't throw that bread out. I don't care how hard it gets. Dunk that in coffee and you have a gourmet meal on your hands."

My dad was a big dunker in his day, and I've followed his path. Like him, I've been known to dip just about anything in coffee—from hard bread to tuna fish sandwiches. Also like him, I enjoy inventing special food combinations. I used to favor the center of a Suzy Q as dip for potato chips. That is, until one day when I heard the center called "spun lard" and that it's supposedly a gray substance dyed white.

Crossing to the living room, I sit in my chair. Pity the hapless person who unknowingly tries to sit in MY CHAIR! And believe me, no one ever sat in my dad's chair—at least without regretting it. To start the day, I'll read my paper and drink my coffee, but if someone dares to interrupt, I'll bark out at them in my dad's gruff morning voice: "What do you want?! What's a matter with you?!" Lord help the person who veered too close to Dad's chair when he was in a mood.

Beside my dad's chair was a table where he kept all his junk. Pens, papers, medicines, Kleenex, bills, "Prize-Word Pete" puzzles he'd always fill out hoping to win the cash prize. Beside *my* bed is a table cluttered with pens, papers, medicines, Kleenex, bills, and much of the same stuff my dad had. (Since my dad fell asleep in the living room a lot, his chair was like his bed.)

Also in my bedroom are dresser drawers that hold books I'll never read, audio tapes I've already listened to, trinkets and bobbles that might be valuable someday, and a velvet pouch containing a gold watch, turquoise pen, Truman button, and various other items I can't part with. My mother kept her drawers the same way. She'd hold on to a cheap piece of jewelry because it had a special clasp on it. A pen that felt good in her hand. A book with a nice binding. "Louie, feel the weight of this pen. And look how well the cover of this book is made . . ." In her private moments, my mother would rummage through her stuff as I sometimes do with my velvet bag.

Heading out into the world, perhaps to get cigarettes as my dad typically did, I find myself imitating his aggressive driving style. He used to drive as if silently chanting the mantra, "I'm the only one on the road. I'm the only one in the world." That was my dad. In his mind, the world didn't really exist without him—and why should it? In some way, he passed along that confidence to me. What makes driving with me even more perilous is that I sometimes find myself drifting off in thought—just as my mom did when she was reminded of her friend Shirley.

*My mom would get on that freeway: twenty, thirty, forty, fifty, fifty, forty, thirty, twenty, she'd slow that car right down.*
*"Shirley lives in that building over there."*
*"Who's Shirley, Mom?"*
*"Oh you know. She's got that crippled chihuahua . . ."*
*I had no idea who Shirley was.*
*My mom wasn't in a lot of accidents, but she sure caused a few of them.*

With both my mom and my dad swirling around in my head while I'm driving, it's amazing I'm still alive.

I could go on, but I think you get my point regarding how much of my parents I carry with me each day—often without realizing it. Consciously or not, we *all* invite our parents along for the ride. So the question underlying our behavior is: Is what we're doing truly self-generated or is it part of "the family matrix"?

Sometimes we call up the unseen forces of our family matrix. We may act a certain way so we can get our imaginary parents to respond to us. I have a friend who's always leaving the cupboard doors open. One day, he realized he was doing that secretly, hoping his mother would come along and shut them. He was forty-two and had his own family, and this behavior drove his wife crazy. Even so, she accepted her lot as her mother-in-law's stand-in, and followed in her husband's wake, making sure those cupboards got closed.

Then there's the woman who constantly criticized her husband—about the way he gave the kids a bath, dragged home late from work, failed to make enough money. The complaints were endless despite the fact that he was clearly trying the best he could. Eventually, she got her husband to ignore her just the way her emotionally distant father ignored her when she was growing up. Why did she engage in such perverse behavior? To her, it was a reflex. By creating with her husband this echo of what had been her childhood experience, she secretly stayed close to her dad.

That's the power of the family matrix.

## FAMILY SURVIVAL TIPS

### (for escaping the family matrix)

**#7 Family cloning.** Realize how much of the life you're living is left over from the life you were raised with. Parents pass down a lot more than we realize. Once we become aware of this, we can start dealing with it. I had a great therapist, Mildred Newman, who once explained to me that a lot of what we do in our present lives is a way of keeping our parents with us. Growing up is realizing we can still keep them in our hearts without repeating the patterns of our childhood.

**#8 DNA (dysfunctional negative attributes).** Some of the stuff that's passed on is better left behind. For example: a tendency to drink, a lack of discipline, a too cynical view of the world. Unlike normal DNA, dysfunctional negative attributes are things we can begin shedding once we realize their origin.

**#9 Get to a phone.** In the movie *The Matrix,* the rebel forces must get to a phone booth to be transported back to "reality." Once on the phone, they're safe. Similarly, all of us need to find lifelines to keep us grounded to a healthier reality. Sometimes this lifeline is a friend, a spouse, or a professional. Don't be afraid to phone for help when you need it.

# Family Reunion

In 1998, while still living in Las Vegas, I was offered a job as host of *Family Feud*. I'd never envisioned myself as a game show host and had concerns. *The Feud* was still widely associated with Richard Dawson. I just couldn't see myself kissing all those contestants like he did. (Giving them a few snacks, *maybe*.) Anyway, I decided to give it a shot.

Around this time I also made another important decision. Instead of running *away* from my family, I decided the solution was to try to *embrace* them. I was on the phone with my brother Frank and I thought it would be nice if all us Anderson siblings got together. I guess what prompted the idea was that Frank was sick—he had chronic heart problems that weren't curable without a transplant, yet he didn't seem all that interested in having one. I'd lost both my parents by this time and who knew how long we'd all be around.

The reunion idea grew from just sisters and brothers getting together to an event that included nieces and nephews. Because I had a deal with Northwest Airlines and a friend at one of the hotels in Las Vegas, the airline and hotel expenses would be somewhat manageable. The proposed get-together kept expanding in size until it included forty-seven Andersons. Okay, it ended up costing an arm and a leg, but hey, isn't this what you should do with fame and fortune?

What a big success and equally big failure the whole thing turned out to be.

Luckily I had some help, but mostly I planned the reunion on my own. I knew the idiosyncrasies of Andersons and realized they'd be less demanding if they dealt with me directly. If I let assistants do it, they'd be easily manipulated by my family. We Andersons are *big* manipulators. I once paid for the repairs on one of my brother's cars only to later learn he didn't even own a car.

So for three days, the forty-seven of us would get together—at Christmas time no less. What could be more fun? Even before it started, I was worried I'd made a big mistake. But sometimes the mistakes you make teach you something. And I'm convinced the positive results of a person's good intentions may not be felt until well after an event.

Below is a copy of the letter each Anderson family member received. For a moment, pretend you're in our extended clan and take a look at what you've won: four fun-filled days in the family-friendly, destination hot spot of the nineties—Las Vegas.

### ANDERSON FAMILY REUNION

*Dear Family and Friends:*

*Here is your information for the Anderson Family Reunion, Las Vegas '98. Enclosed is your flight information. All tickets must be picked up at the airline counter at least one and a half hours before the flight takes off. A picture I.D. is required.*

*Enclosed is cab fare from the airport to the Luxor Hotel. This is where you'll be staying. When you arrive at the Luxor Hotel (it's the Pyramid), go to the front desk. Be patient, your room has been reserved. You'll need a picture I.D. Enclosed is your room reservation list. Your confirmation number is next to your name.*

*Enclosed is your activity schedule, which will tell you what we have planned. Please read over the details carefully. If something doesn't go perfectly, don't panic. Remember, everyone makes mistakes. Because there are almost sixty of you (a few more got added in) please take this into consideration before you fall to pieces or jump to conclusions.*

*I am very excited to see everyone. Remember, this is going to be a fun time for all of us. One more thing: Enclosed is a Priority Mail stamped envelope. This is so you can send me photos of your family. Please write the names of the people in the pictures plus ages on the back of each photo. I need these for a special project I am slaving over [a documentary I have been working on for years about, what else—my family]. Again, I can't wait to see you all!!! Have a safe trip.*

Sounds nice enough, doesn't it? Or are you smarter than me and can see it all coming? I'm hoping you're getting the chance here to live vicariously through a family reunion without having to actually experience the downside—e.g., the embarrassment of commenting on how great your aunt Martha's hair looks only to be told it's a wig, or listening to your uncle Ernie as he tries to get you to invest in his latest invention, "the pocket bladder," which turns out to be a hot water bottle you can pee into when you go hunting.

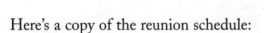

Here's a copy of the reunion schedule:

*Friday, December 18<sup>th</sup>: Everyone arrives in Las Vegas and checks into the Luxor Hotel. This is your time to settle in and relax. There are no planned activities for this day. Sleep well. Saturday, December 19<sup>th</sup>: Everyone is invited to see the Louie Anderson Show at the Monte Carlo Hotel in the Lance Burton Theater. Showtime is 8:00 P.M. Sunday, December 20<sup>th</sup>: Dinner and celebration at 6:00 P.M. at the Excalibur Hotel. Monday, December 21<sup>st</sup>: Time to head home. Boo hoo! Everyone cries. But don't despair because Louie is already busy planning next year's reunion. Thanks for coming. I love you all very much and will miss you. Have a safe trip home.*

Well, you can see how full of hope and optimism I was. Of course, that was coupled with a strange feeling of dread. What *is* it about family reunions that fills us with such mixed emotions? Is it because these are the people who know us best, and thus know all our vulnerabilities? Is it because we nourish the often dashed hope that something will be solved?

Even the term "family reunion" is a strange thing. If you're already a family, why do you need reuniting?

I think people come to family reunions looking for different ways of seeing themselves and measuring how they're doing in relation to everyone else. *Oh, there's Cousin Earl who still doesn't have a job and is missing two teeth from his latest bar fight. At least I'm doing better than him. Thank goodness I stayed in school.* Or *There's Grandpa Johnson—he doesn't look bad for eighty, and hey, he still has it with the ladies. That's who I want to be when I get old.* Or maybe *There's crazy Aunt Connie wearing that surgical mask because she's still afraid of hotel germs. At least I've got it more together than her.*

Other folks come to reunions thinking it will solve a problem. *This time I'll get the respect I deserve—especially when I rent the Caddie and make sure everyone sees me valet park it out front.* Of course, this problem solving rarely happens since relatives can be kind of like the folks in the Middle East. There's such a long history of hurts and wounds that the most insignificant slight can set off a skirmish. At such times, to make *any* comment is like walking through a minefield. Dialogue in situations like this tends to come with subtitles.

"Hey, Uncle Paulie, great to see you."

*(I'm only saying hi because Grandma Gertrude made me, she's old and I don't want to get cut out of her will.)*

"How's my favorite nephew, Andy? You liking the new job?"

*(When are you going to pay me back the money you owe me, bum?)*

"Terrific. So, you're looking good. New haircut."

*(Give the comb-over a rest for Pete's sake.)*

"Well, I've been exercising."

*(I've been watching more ESPN.)*

"It shows. You know, we should really get together and play some golf."

*(Maybe you'll keel over on the third hole and I won't have to pay you the money I owe you.)*

"Definitely. Call me and I'll take you over to the country club."

*(Thank goodness I have caller I.D. with privacy plus.)*

Well, maybe that's a little harsh, but you get the idea.

• • •

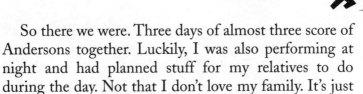

So there we were. Three days of almost three score of Andersons together. Luckily, I was also performing at night and had planned stuff for my relatives to do during the day. Not that I don't love my family. It's just that, like any good thing—you can get *too* much.

During this time, the *Family Feud* people asked me if after one of my Vegas shows, I'd persuade some audience members to play the game with me onstage so they could tape it as a sales tool. The new set wasn't finished yet and we needed some footage to show the television syndicators at NAPTE, the convention where they sell TV shows to the folks who put them on the air locally. I agreed to do these test shows using an old set they had, but said, "Hey, why not use (you can see this mistake coming, can't you?) *my* family?" (If for some strange reason you ever find yourself in my position, don't do this. Even though I didn't pick who should play the game, many of my family members are *still* mad at me for not making sure they were chosen.) So I wound up taping the first primitive episodes of *Family Feud* with my actual family. Not only was that tape shown to station owners around the country and helped sell the show, but more than that, it captured a magical moment. It was certainly one of the high points of the reunion.

One night was devoted to food, fun, four weddings (some people actually decided to get married during this occasion), and, of course, Santa. I know how much we Andersons like our presents. There was even a performance by another Anderson, my nephew Justin, who's a great country pop singer.

I arrived a short time after the party started, having headed there right after my show. It was amazing to see

how little the gene pool varied in our family. Boy, we all looked alike. I made my rounds, talked with everyone, and took a million photos—and there was a wonderful toast in which my oldest brother Frank thanked me.

That there'd been four weddings that night excited me, but then someone approached me about shelling out for the minister. I know this is silly, especially when I'd spent so much on everything else, but I was bothered by the *expectation*—the sense of entitlement. Additionally, a couple of siblings asked for gambling cash or came to me with sob stories explaining why they needed more money, which further darkened my mood. Instead of enjoying the event—instead of just *being* there as one of several siblings—I felt thrust into the role of parent. Why couldn't I be like everyone else—just some guy who shows up and enjoys the party?

Maybe I was overreacting, but as my family members approached me with various problems, I started to feel like it was my job to solve them. Not that I hadn't, in a sense, set myself up by throwing this reunion in the first place. But suddenly I wasn't the Louie I wanted to be; I was the Louie they all saw me as. At least, that's the way I perceived it. I bit my tongue, made a last round of good-byes and said good night.

I remember going to family events as a kid that my rich uncle would attend. People used to hate him. "That friggin' guy could help us out if he wanted to," they'd mutter under their breaths as he said good night. I've always tried to be generous with my family. But sometimes I feel like I've become my hated rich uncle. I get the feeling they think I could always do more.

By the reunion's end I was glad to have it over with and wanted to get as far away from my guests as I could. Am I alone in this overwhelming longing to be with my family coupled with an intense desire to get away from them? Why am I so sensitive to requests from family members? In the end, does it boil down to a fear that I'm not loved for myself, for who I really am, but for the success machine I've become?

I do recognize in myself that Anderson insatiability, that feeling of always wanting more. Part of what I'm working on now is my ability to deal with disappointments, to not let them get to me so much.

Maybe family reunions would work out better if they were just twenty minutes. You could all meet at the airport, have one drink, and then everybody would go home.

"How are you?"

"Great."

"How are you?"

"Great."

"Nice seeing you."

"You too."

"We should do this more often."

"Definitely."

"See you next year."

"Will do."

Then people could spend the five hours on the way home discussing that twenty minutes.

"Could you believe Aunt Helen got a face-lift? She still looks old . . ."

"Uncle Al's such a bastard, isn't he? He acts all nice toward me, but I know he hates my guts."

"And how about that Jennifer Lopez dress she was wearing?! Please, who wants to see that?"

In the end, I'm still glad I organized that reunion. The main reason for doing it was to give a sense of possibility to my nephews and nieces, along with an idea of who their family is and where they come from. Maybe I want them to have the sense of history and identity I've spent my adult life looking for. Would I do it again? Yes, but next time I'd probably do it differently.

## FAMILY SURVIVAL TIPS
### (for family functions)

**#10 Always keep an eye on your emotional fuel tank.** Before going to a family function, think beforehand of how to ensure that you survive it intact. Assess the amount of emotional energy the event is likely to draw from your personal fuel tank. Allow one gallon to get to the actual event. Another to get there on time. Another because you'll be seeing your cousin Derek—the one who always flaunts his new promotion to try to make you feel like a loser. And, finally, another gallon for unexpected family land mines such as Uncle Luke who hasn't been taking his medication and is making you call him "General" as he gives orders to the troops in Afghanistan from his cell phone. Most important, leave enough gas to get home safely. You can do this by

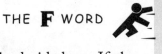

exiting at a time you've previously decided on. If the party is from three to six, arrive at three-thirty and leave at five. You don't want to be the first to show up or the last to go. And you may want to call Cousin Derek before the event and congratulate him on becoming vice president of everything-important-in-the-universe.

**#11 Don't be a nuclear reactor.** Families know how to get to you. Your job is to learn how to *respond*, not *react*. They may be fishing, but you don't have to take the bait. Just as some people can be on a desert island, but in a mental sense, be totally surrounded by family, some people can be in the middle of a reunion and yet remain apart from how their family defines them.

**#12 Family subtitles.** Keep an ear open for what's *really* being said. You don't have to respond to each subtle assault, but at least monitor how you're feeling as the zingers come your way. Always ask yourself *why*. If Cousin Derek's seemingly innocent comment about the car you're driving bothers you, there's probably something there and you should pay attention to it.

**#13 Check your baggage before the flight.** You can't help bringing an agenda to a family meeting like this. You're only human. But realize nothing will ge resolved during the event and let everything go.

**#14 Family prepping.** You know how, when you bring a new person to meet your family, you first warn them that Uncle Harry makes offensive, off-color jokes and that Aunt Nancy is a witch who isn't happy until she cuts everyone down to size? Give yourself the same advisory. Prep yourself as if you were that stranger.

# Family I.Q.

After that family reunion experience, I realized that fostering family solidarity isn't as simple as getting everybody in one room and trying to make nice. I knew I had to look more deeply at families. And to help me do that, I've devised my own family I.Q. test.

Before we start, a short pop quiz: What exactly is a family? The word itself derives from the Latin *familia,* meaning "servant." *Servant?* As in "get the paper," "grab that remote control for me," "take out the garbage"? Ah, finally it all makes sense.

Below is a set of questions designed to make you aware of how conscious you are of your own family. You can't fail this test. You can only fail your family.

Just kidding!

**1) When people ask "How's your family?" what's your response?**
**a)** Great.
**b)** Okay, I guess.
**c)** Don't ask.
**d)** I hate my family.
**e)** Buried under the garage, if you must know.

**2) When asked "How's your family?" which of the below describes what you're** *thinking:*

**a)** I'll say "great" because it is great.

**b)** I'll say "great" because that's what I've learned to say.

**c)** I'll say "okay" and add "I guess" to see if the questioner cares enough to press further.

**d)** I'll say "don't ask me about my family" because it's none of their business, and if they press, they'll get an earful.

**e)** I'll say "I hate my family" because it will either shut this person up, make them laugh, or get them to mirror my answer with "Yeah, I hate my family too."

**3) Compared to your friends' families, how would you rate your relationship with your family?**

**a)** Great.

**b)** Pretty good.

**c)** About the same.

**d)** Much worse.

**e)** Unbearable.

**f)** Hopeless.

**4) Answer the following questions using a scale of 1–10 in which 10 is the best:**

**a)** How happy is your family? \_\_\_\_

**b)** How honest is your family? \_\_\_\_

**c)** How close is your family? \_\_\_\_

**5) Which TV family is most like yours?**

**a)** The family in *Roseanne*.

**b)** The family in *Everybody Loves Raymond*.

**c)** The family in *Married . . . with Children.*
**d)** The family in *The Sopranos.*

**6) What is your family's favorite holiday?**
**a)** Christmas, Hanukkah, or Kwanzaa.
**b)** Thanksgiving.
**c)** Fourth of July.
**d)** Arbor Day.

**7) How truthful (which is something different from honest) is your family?**
**a)** Very.
**b)** Pretty.
**c)** Not very.
**d)** All liars but me.
**e)** All liars.

**8) Does most of your family still live close to where you grew up?**
**a)** Most still do.
**b)** Some do, but some of us wouldn't if we had the opportunity to move.
**c)** We're spread out because of employment or school.
**d)** We stay as far away from each other as possible.

**9) What best describes your type of family?**
**a)** Parents only married once to each other and still together.
**b)** Divorced and not speaking to each other.
**c)** Divorced and still speaking.
**d)** Divorced but remarried to other people.
**e)** One or both parents deceased.

**10) Do you consider friends more your family than your own flesh and blood?**
a) Yes.
b) No.

Now, this isn't the SATs. There are no grades. But let's take each question in turn and look at what we can learn from the answers.

### QUESTION #1. When people ask "How's your family?" what's your response?

I'm surprised by the number of people who've never even thought about how they answer that question. Most tell me they answer "b"—"okay, I guess." Did they not answer "a" because they feel there's always something in relationships that can be improved? Or did they answer "okay, I guess" because they long to have someone to talk over their family situation with? Many of us are uncomfortable discussing family with other people. It's that old adage "what goes on in this family, stays in this family." Or if you're a *Godfather* fan, it's that scene where Marlon Brando slaps around James Caan for letting outsiders know what the family is thinking.

In theory, we're supposed to solve problems within our own family. But when I talk with people, I sense family issues weigh on them so heavily that they're willing to resolve them by any means necessary.

### QUESTION #2. When asked "How's your family?" which of the below describes what you're *thinking*:

The follow-up question is meant to give people a chance to clarify and think more deeply about why they answer the way they do about their families. I must admit, I tend to not trust people who say their families are great. You mean, there's *nothing* you'd like to change? If that's the truth, please write me care of the publisher. Why *is* your family so great? It needs to be studied by scientists.

Okay, so I'm being cynical. I do know there are many good families out there.

**QUESTION #3. Compared to your friends' families, how would you rate your relationship with your family?**

Most people I informally surveyed said their family was about the same or better than their friends' families. That may be because we all have two groups of friends. The first group I call our "perfect friends"—those whom we aspire to be like. For example: Rob and Jill, both physicians who do a lot of charity work, but never miss daughter Crystal's dance recital or son Trevor's swim meet, and take great pride in listing the numerous academic honors their kids have collected.

The second group of friends is, shall we say, "less than perfect." You know, people like your buddy Jake from high school who has two strikes against him because he keeps getting into cars that aren't his and saying "Oh, I thought it was *my* car." He and his wife, Lee Anne, have nine children, due to Jake's refusal to get a vasectomy. And Lee Anne has been on disability since she hurt her back hooking up the propane to their double-wide trailer. Jake and Lee Ann are the kinds of friends you keep to reassure yourself you're doing just fine.

QUESTION #4. How happy, honest, and close is your family on a scale of 1–10 in which 10 is the best?

When rating their families, most people answer with sixes and sevens. Once again, they believe their families are okay, but could use improvement. One person rated her family a ten. Wow. I want to move in with them!

QUESTION #5. Which TV family is most like yours?

In the show *Roseanne*, the husband and wife have their problems but still love each other. If you compared your family to the family on that show, you likely have a realistic sense of how most families are: dysfunctional but doing the best they can. If you picked *Everybody Loves Raymond*, you're probably in pretty good shape. Your family is endearingly dysfunctional, and things always end up working out in the end. If you picked the *Married . . . with Children* brood, there's still time to get on *The Jerry Springer Show*. If you picked *The Sopranos*, you don't have to worry about your family because you'll be dead soon.

QUESTION #6. What is your family's favorite holiday?

If you like Christmas or Thanksgiving, you're interested in resolving things with your family. Certainly, if you picked Thanksgiving, your family is functional enough for you to look forward to spending a meal with them. Congratulations! If you picked Christmas, it may be because Christmas was a happy time in your childhood. (Or maybe you're simply the type of person who can be bribed with nicely wrapped gifts.) Be aware that the way you've handled recent Christmases may have been an attempt—perhaps a *failed* attempt—to re-create that happy time in your past. Fourth of July is usually reserved for those with a more independent spirit—which can be healthy. Fans of the Fourth like to get together over the summer when the number of things going on usually takes the pressure off the occasion.

If you picked Arbor Day, well, no more need be said.

### QUESTION #7. How truthful is your family?

Just because your family is honest doesn't mean they're truthful. Sometimes a family skates by on superficialities. A truthful family goes deeper and tries to get at what's going on. Just by asking this question, I find I get people thinking harder about what's true in their family.

### QUESTION #8. Does most of your family still live close to where you grew up?

Have you moved away because you want to break free of your family? Have you stayed close by because it was your choice or out of guilt? Are you close to home because you're enjoying the process of working out family problems?

Sometimes we're aware of why we are where we are, and sometimes we aren't. Have you abandoned your family physically? Emotionally? Be honest.

### QUESTION #9. What best describes your type of family?

If your parents are still together and in a decent relationship, you'll have a tendency to stay together because that's your model. If you grew up the product of a messy

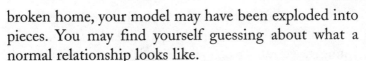

broken home, your model may have been exploded into pieces. You may find yourself guessing about what a normal relationship looks like.

I have a friend whose parents never spoke after they got divorced. For the next ten years, his father referred to his mother only as "that woman." My friend didn't have a relationship all through high school. Then he went out to California to meet his uncle and aunt who'd been happily married for twenty years. Discovering that relationships *could* work, my friend came back and got involved with his first girlfriend. Ironically, a few weeks later, his aunt and uncle filed for divorce.

Not all divorces are devastating. As long as you've seen some relationship working, there's hope and a trail to follow. If not, you need to find your own path.

If your parents are gone, you may have accepted the role of parent to your siblings and become more responsible than is healthy. You may regret not having your mom and dad to turn to and ask questions of. Because of our tendency to make those who aren't with us saints or sinners, you may end up romanticizing relationships, or conversely, projecting your leftover anger onto your current situation. Always remember that your relationship is with your present family and not with your absent parents.

QUESTION #10. **Do you consider friends more your family than your own flesh and blood?**

Often, I find that people's great need for family will drive them to create a familylike connection with their friends. Those with non-nurturing home lives are especially drawn to these surrogate relationships. Sometimes people choose as friends those who resemble real-life family members—hopefully, with the annoying habits not present. Unfortunately, particularly when we're younger, we tend to choose friends whose traits match exactly those we were exposed to in the home environment, because they're familiar.

## FAMILY SURVIVAL TIP

### (for those afraid of failing the test)

#15 Examine thyself. Don't be afraid to look at your feelings toward your family in a new way. Family I.Q. is different from the kind of intelligence that enables a person to know what an isosceles triangle is, but just as important. Trust me, in real life family issues will crop up more than geometry problems. Don't worry whether you passed or failed, just keep asking questions.

# Family Morning Rituals

*(Me at the family breakfast table staring across from my younger brother Mikey.)*

*"Everyone is mad at you. Dad is mad at you. Mom is mad at you. All the kids at school—they're mad at you too. The people at the mall—mad at you. The farmers out in Hinkley—mad at you. The whole world is mad at you. Dad, aren't you mad at him?"*

*(Dad, walking in, oblivious.) "Damn right, I'm mad at him."*

*"See, told you."*

*My dad to Frank: "Shut up!"*
*Frank to me: "Shut up!"*
*Me to Mikey: "Shut up! You know, you're ruining this whole family."*

This dialogue is just one example of how we Andersons would torture each other as the day began. What was going on? Morning for us was like the plains of the African Serengeti. Just as the steam rises up from the grasslands, you'd see it coming off our oatmeal. The bacon my mom put down at the table would provoke the same kind of feeding frenzy as when a pride of lions spots a wounded gazelle. And there definitely was a hierarchy. My dad would eat first, followed by the strongest and the fittest. Little brothers would be like hyenas picking up after scraps.

Part of what was going on was that Dad was going out into a cruel world he had no control over. He'd take it out on Mom who'd get nervous and be short with one of us kids who, in turn, would inflict it on the person they had control over. Mikey, being the youngest, had to wait to find some kid on the way to school before he could get *his* revenge.

## FAMILY SURVIVAL TIP
### (for the A.M.)

**#16 Don't take your morning out on your family.** Yes, the world can be a cruel place. But our families are supposed to be a sanctuary from that. I have a friend who in the morning was being very annoying with his wife and daughter, making obnoxious noises and saying ridiculous things. So one morning his wife took a tape recorder and taped him. The next day, she played it back to him. When he heard how absurd he sounded, he thought twice about acting that way again.

# Family History

A fellow comedian once joked, "No one has made more money off their unhappy childhood than Louie Anderson." The truth is, my childhood—like everyone's—was complex. And the things that affected me started way before I was born. I've spent a lot of time thinking about my past and researching where I came from.

You need to know the past so you can deal with it. Unlike me, you may not have written two books about your parents and created an animated a version of your youth as I did with my cartoon *Life with Louie,* but I'm sure certain stories have been passed down to you. As I talk here about *my* background, I hope it will inspire you to dig more deeply into *your* origins.

## Father's Footsteps

Someone once observed that those siblings who looked most like my dad are the ones who ended up the craziest. Crazy and genius. They always seem to go together, don't they? If you've heard my act, watched my cartoon, or read *Dear Dad,* my father probably needs no introduction. He's the irascible guy who sat around in his uniform—undershirt and boxers—spouting off about the world from his La-Z-Boy.

*"Dad, we're having company. Do you think you could put some pants on?"*

*"I don't care if the president's coming over. If he starts paying the rent, then I'll put some pants on."*

You may have heard my line about wishing Dad smoked pot instead of drank. Then maybe he would have talked to me about the latest Zeppelin albums instead of saying things like:

*"Lou-eee! Do you see that? Those neighbors—they keep moving their house closer to ours!"*

I've made a nice living just repeating his unique brand of logic.

*While he was driving:*
*"If I was the last man on earth, some moron would turn left in front of me."*

Underneath the jokes, my dad was a complicated figure. We never really know who our parents are. In researching *Dear Dad*, I discovered that Dad had a soft side that was pretty much invisible by the time I came along. I found love letters he'd written to my mother in which he endearingly called her "Toy." I also discovered one of the reasons he'd been so harsh to us all those years. When he was young, he was sent off to live with a cold foster family who treated him as a farm slave and worked him all the time. He was made to sleep in the unheated attic. When they passed the food around at dinner, my father wasn't allowed to have seconds unless everyone else in the family had eaten as much as they wanted. But in looking further into his background for this book, I've discovered even more about him.

My father's father, Alfred Anderson, invented the clothespin. Don't believe me? Here's the patent:

**773,449. CLOTHES-CLAMP.** ALFRED ANDERSON, Detroit City, Minn., assignor of three-fourths to Asahel G. Wedge, Halvor Rasmusson, and Peter K. Haslerud, Detroit City, Minn. Filed Mar. 3, 1904. Serial No. 196,340. (No model.)

*Claim.*—A clothes-clamping device comprising a single piece of wire bent about intermediate its ends to form a supporting-loop, said wire being extended laterally from the supporting-loop to form a shank and downwardly projected from the shank and formed into flared spring clamp members, the said clamp members comprising spaced elements of the wire, said wire being extended upwardly from the clamp members and formed into finger-pieces disposed in diverged relation, one of the extremities of the wire being bent to embrace the shank, the other extremity being projected between the clamp members to form a stop.

He also invented seventy other items, some of which we still use in our daily lives.

Pretty clever, huh? That's the genius part. The insane part was that he sold the patent for the clip clothespin for $500. Must have seemed like a lot back then. He also filed patents for his version of the stove hood, a railway switch, a mechanism for opening and closing doors, and a deep fryer. If he'd been a little better at business, we all might be as rich as the Gettys or the Rockefellers.

Then again, I probably wouldn't have become a stand-up comic. Not many sons and daughters of magnates are funny. It's hard for an audience to identify with jokes about denting the Rolls-Royce Corniche your dad gave you for your sixteenth birthday, or about being paid an allowance in long-term T-bills.

For a while, my dad's future was full of promise. He played the trumpet for Hoagy Carmichael's band. (Hoagy, who wrote "Stardust," was a cool cat—the Sting of his day.) But as the kids piled up, it became impossible to stay on the road all the time. My dad tried to get a more responsible job, but it wasn't in him and he started drinking more and more.

I think back to when my mom and dad had their first child. When a family is starting, there are such high hopes. *Maybe my kid will grow up to be president. We're going to do things different from our parents. Be closer.* People start off with the best of intentions. But somehow along the way even the most well-laid plans get screwed up, and demons come to haunt us.

# Fossils

In every family, there are secrets that lie buried. As I mentioned, my theory for why my father was so bitter was that he was put up for adoption. (By the way, the term "put up" harks back to a time before adoption agencies when kids were "put up" before church to see if anyone from the congregation would like to take them home.) Only recently did I discover that my father's parents were forced to give him up after an incident with his older sister Olga and the Swedish mafia.

I'm not kidding—this is the truth, as I've heard it.

Apparently, Olga was baby-sitting and threw a party during which a Swedish gang showed up and killed someone. My grandparents had no knowledge of what had gone on, but when the authorities looked into it, they declared my grandparents unfit guardians and forced them to give my father up to foster care. This series of events, hidden from me for my first forty-five years, probably triggered much of my father's behavior and left aftershocks that my family is *still* dealing with.

So the whole destiny of the Anderson family was changed by Swedish gangs. Yes, Swedish gangs. What were they like, I wonder. Instead of the Crips and

Bloods, were they the Fjords and the Smorgasbords? I can just picture a Swedish gang leader named Sven chatting up his troops in a turf war with those bad-assed Norwegians. "Okay, here's dah plan, ya. Ve open de front der. Ollie and Gunther, dey will cover de back. And den we get that big Norwegian and we tell heim, stay oudda our feeshing area. De herring are ours. Ere's how we start. Olef will drive the dogsled and den Ingabord will follow with the reindeer wagon. Ven de door opens, they come out on the porch, ya. I'll drop the mackerel net and we'll get that big Nordski. Den Lars will hold the harpoon gun on de big goon. And if ve don't get what ve want, he'll be fish bait."

The truth is, most of us are crazy people raised by crazy people who were raised by crazy people. In caveman time, it was probably no better. Back then, my dad would have been tipsy from drinking too much red berry juice and complaining that my mom overcooked the pterodactyl.

## Females
### (thank God for moms)

My mother's side of the family was a little more stable. She grew up well-to-do. Her father owned a fleet of gas stations. He was a kind man who so loved children that he made the windows on their house lower so that his little kids could look out the front windows and see everything. During the Great Depression, when everyone was hit hard, he extended credit to all his customers who couldn't pay for gas. But when the Depression was over, no one paid him back. He never got over that. My mother always said he died of a broken heart.

My mother's ancestors, the Windsors, dated all the way back to the Pilgrims. They came over on the *Mayflower* and were probably there for the first Thanksgiving. You think that Thanksgiving was any different from the ones we have today? I can just see my mom's great-great-great grandmother pushing her favorite dishes on those Native Americans. "Oh, come on, Chief, try a little of my sweet potatoes. They've got marshmallows on top." We'll never know exactly what was said at that first Thanksgiving, but if the families who celebrated it were anything like families these days, I'm sure there were some harsh words and hurt feelings. It's easy to imagine how the uprisings started between the settlers and the Indians.

# Finding Each Other

So how did my mom and dad meet? The only account we really have is from my mother. My dad didn't talk about things like that much. Anyway, my mom's story is that she showed up at one of my dad's gigs, the Corn Palace Festival in Mitchell, South Dakota. Back then, big band music was all the rage and people drove for miles to hear it played. My mother was a little overweight, but she knew how to get the boys over to her car. She always kept packs of cigarettes in the backseat.

My mother's family was dead set against my mother going out with my father. After all, he was a *musician*— a trumpet player. My mother had a stubborn streak, though, and she ended up with my dad. He'd been married once before and it's unclear exactly when he got a divorce (pre- or post my mom), but thankfully, there were no kids involved.

Granted, I've spent my adult life making fun of how horrible my father—and sometimes, even my mother— could be. Despite that, though, I believe that their marriage of forty-plus years was essentially a happy one.

My mom was devastated when Dad passed away in 1979 and, after that, whenever she'd come to my shows,

she'd fold her arms across herself whenever I talked about Dad onstage. She must have still been in love with him. (Whenever I'd do material about *her*, she'd smile and say afterward, "I guess I *am* a little like that.") I try to remind myself that I came along in my parents' marriage after they'd already had nine children so I didn't get to witness much romance between them. They were mostly just tired. Sometimes people who hear that I'm from a family of eleven kids ask if we were Catholic. No, I tell them, my dad was a musician.

Each one of my brothers and sisters came along at a different point in my family's history. But the fact is, we Anderson kids all had the same parents. So the question remains, how did I end up getting out, making it to *The Tonight Show* and beyond?

## FAMILY SURVIVAL TIP

### (for you history majors)

**#17 The past is not dead—it's not even yet past.** Whether you choose to accept it or not, you're a product of your family's history. The question is, what chapter are you going to write next? What part are you going to take with you and what part are you going to leave behind? Will you be the one to break away from the family pattern? Or, like some tragic figure, are you destined to repeat parts of what haunted your parents? I avoided my dad's drinking, but of course, ended up replacing it with food. Defying your family's history is tricky business.

# Family Soup

## (nature vs. nurture, how did I get out?)

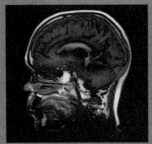 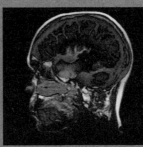 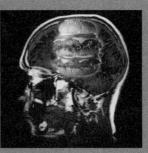

**Normal Brain**  **Schizophrenic Brain**  **Anderson Brain**

One was a criminal. One was a paranoid schizophrenic. One was a drifter. One had a job cleaning a bowling alley. No, it's not an episode of *Survivor*. It's my family. In the last chapter, I asked what made me different. Of the eleven kids who grew up in the projects in Minnesota, what was it that allowed me to become so successful (at least in one specific area)? Was it some weird gene I had that the others lacked? Or did I get something from my upbringing—from being the second to last on the scene—that the others didn't? Perhaps I simply inherited a favorable mix of traits from my parents: my father's artistry and my mother's stability and tenacity.

Every one of my siblings has special qualities—intelligence, compassion, humor—and some have probably lived more fulfilling lives. But because I wound up with the money and fame, like it or not I've been singled out.

## FBI

Actually, my oldest brother Frank was famous way before me. Of course, it was for being a criminal. But he made the paper and the FBI came to our house. If *America's Most Wanted* had been around back then, Frank might have inspired several episodes.

Seriously, Frank is a bright guy. But being the oldest, he was the one who took the brunt of my father's belt. He got hit. That's got to affect a guy. By the time I came along, my dad was fifty. That means when I was ten, he was sixty. Maybe he *wanted* to beat me, but his arthritis would flair up and he thought better of it. (That would make an interesting aspirin commercial. Setup: Images of a drunk dad looking to whack his kid, but being stymied by his arthritis. Voiceover: "Does this happen to you? Pop a couple of Bayer and you can whack away.")

Allow me to share one example of my brother Frank's criminal creativity. He coated steel bars with sterling silver plating so that they'd look like *real* silver. Then, having learned how to print in the prison workshop, he created an article that said silver bars had been stolen from a train robbery in Boston. He then sold the fake silver bars, telling people to bury the bars in their back-yards till the caper cooled off. By the time his customers became suspicious, he was long gone.

Then there's my brother Kyle. Third eldest, he was the spitting image of my dad and my father's favorite. Growing up, my brother Frank used to call Kyle "the squealer." When they skipped school, Kyle was the first to tell our dad. I guess things never change, because when Frank heisted some rifles, Kyle helped turn Frank in. (We later discovered Kyle was involved in the incident and had squealed to keep out of jail.) Kyle's behavior was also most like my dad's. Sadly, he ended up following in his footsteps and became a drinker who wasn't always so nice to his kids. (Later, he stopped drinking and developed a better relationship with his children.)

Like me, you've probably heard stories of people choosing spouses who exhibit their parents' worst tendencies. Does genetic programming foreordain these choices? Are these folks trying to re-create the home they grew up in? We've all heard tales of identical twins separated at birth who meet each other forty years later and are both chain-smoking, beer-guzzling, dog-racing fans—even though one was raised in the projects and one was adopted by a billionaire. Something of the sort happened to my sister Sally. Because of the financial problems my parents were wrestling with, at six months old, Sally was sent to live with our rich Uncle Ike and Aunt Iona in South Dakota. I was always sad that happened. But trust me, despite my mother's sister largely raising her, Sally is still 100 percent Anderson with all our charms and flaws.

## Food for Thought

I was contemplating the mysteries of all this family stuff one night on the road, eating bad Chinese food outside Detroit, Michigan. As I was reflecting on some of the stories I've shared with you, I started to ask more questions: What is it about family that has such hold over us? Is it genetic? Is it environmental? How is it different if you're the oldest? The youngest? Would you still be the same person if you came from a totally different

family? Has the "idea" of family changed much over the years?

That's when the answer hit me like the hardened wonton I was trying to bite into: Families are a lot like soup. The same ingredients can be thrown into the same pot and yet the results can be different each time. Sometimes the soup is cooked at a higher temperature. Other times it's left on the stove too long and takes on a different texture and consistency. Perhaps too much salt was added or the carrots weren't as fresh.

There are times, of course, when the soup comes out just perfect and you remember the taste for the rest of your life. Even if you made the perfect soup once though, because there are so many factors involved in its preparation, it's unlikely you'll be able to make it the same way again.

So *how* are families like soup? First, they need to be watched over during all stages of their development. Second, the availability of good ingredients is crucial. For example, how well are your parents able to support your physical, spiritual, and emotional needs? Third, much depends on when you were taken out of the pot. If you were born in the beginning of a marriage when everything was great, that will affect you differently than if your dad just lost his job.

Let me put it this way: We're all soup of the day. What day we came out of the pot determines to a large extent whom we'll be—both as a family member and future family soup maker.

In trying to figure out where I came from, I started by examining the particular ingredients in *my* family soup. In a lot of ways, my dad was the spice, and my mom, the sturdy base that held everything together. But there are more factors than just that. So, in the chapters that follow, I'll take a look at them—such things as family genes, family placement (where in the family I came from), and family environment.

After I'd finished my contemplative meal of bad Chinese, I opened my stale fortune cookie. It warned, "Beware of looking foolish."

Oh well, here goes . . .

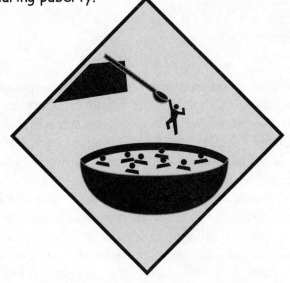

## RECIPE FOR ANDERSON FAMILY SOUP

2½ quarts family genes
3 cups family environment
1 pint family placement
Dash of dysfunction
Pinch of codependency

Simmer through childhood, bring to a boil during puberty.

# Family Genes

*My mother ate butter her whole life. She had to have butter with everything. We'd be in restaurants and she'd say, "We'd like some extra butter. Can we have some extra butter, please?" and the host would say, "Could you wait till we seat your party first, ma'am?" My mom ate every piece of butter in the Midwest and yet lived till she was seventy-seven. My father smoked and drank his whole life. At seventy-nine, we finally had to kill him.*

Those are jokes from my act, but there's some truth to it all. Some people inherit family constitutions so weak that a simple pat of butter combined with a brisk jog induces a heart attack, while others are a bit different. It seems like you could pour lard directly into an Anderson's veins and we'd keep going.

Every week it seems we hear about a scientist isolating a different gene. This one controls eating, this one controls hair loss, this one controls whether you chew your tongue like a cow and make strange moaning sounds when you wake up in the morning. I look at genes as belonging to two categories: There are one's family genes, and genes that get passed along just by virtue of being a Homo sapien.

Now, remember, I'm no scientist. I sometimes do this bit in my act about my father saying to me when he was a kid, "There were no schools. You had to find smart people and follow them around." The routine continues with me, as child-Louie, uttering a smart-mouthed reply, and my father threatening me.

Me: "Guess you never found anyone, huh?"

My dad: "Hey, I heard that. You want to walk home from here?"

Me: "Sure, why not? We're in the garage."

Anyway, much like my father, I've tried to hang out with some smart people and read a few books, and along the way I've developed a few theories.

Apparently, there's a nut in the front of the brain, a lump of certain types of cells, that functions as an early warning system. If people were cartoons, this nut would be like a flashing red light, warning DANGER when we're about to do something that could be harmful. In my case, the warning light seems to work for, say, skydiving, but it is a bit defective when it comes to, say, French fries. Similarly, some people seem to have diminished warning systems for drugs or alcohol, making them prone to addiction. The great thing about becoming aware of your genetic makeup is that you can then try to do something about it. If you know how your brain is programmed, you can deprogram it.

Unfortunately, acquiring information about your genetic programming isn't as easy as getting an X ray. Wouldn't it be great if when a person passed through airport security, he could just lay down with his carry-on luggage and have the technician give him a scan. "Yes,

Mr. Anderson, it seems like your genetic structure pre-disposes you to eating every Mrs. Field's cookie in sight. To avoid the cookie and donut shops take concourse C."

According to a book called *Mean Genes,* there's actu-ally a gene that causes us to spend our resources. Back when people didn't have the ability to preserve food, they were forced to use it or lose it. This genetic need to spend explains why we're always running up credit-card bills, not to mention America's growing fascination with gambling and five-dollar café lattes. It's just not our nature to save. That's for squirrels.

In my Vegas act, I coax uncomfortable laughs from the audience when I say, "You're never going to win. Look how big this casino is, look how big your house is. Figure it out." I joke about the guys who blow thou-sands of dollars on the casino floor and return to their rooms at three in the morning to face wives who scold them for not wanting to spend ninety bucks on Siegfried and Roy tickets. But after my act's over, what do I do? The same thing I warned my audience about.

The odds being what they are, I might as well stand in the middle of the casino floor, toss my money into the air, then go get a ninety-nine-cent scrambled egg break-fast. The question is: Knowing all I do, why do I gamble like this? Are human beings prone to this weakness? Or is it the Anderson genes specifically? Does it have some-thing to do with the way I was raised? Is it because my dad took me to play bingo with him?

That's what I'm on a quest to find out.

## FAMILY SURVIVAL TIP

### (for swimming around in your gene pool)

**#18 Know what genes you're wearing.** Scientists say if one identical twin suffers from schizophrenia, there's a 50 to 60 percent chance the other twin will also have the disease. I've heard that the child of an alcoholic has a 50 percent chance of becoming a drinker himself. Environment probably plays a big role in this, but you've got to believe that genes are heavily implicated in people's problems. One day we'll all probably carry our genetic code on a card in our pocket. Until then, make a point to observe your family and deduce what genes you've inherited. Even if you sense you have a genetic predisposition, that doesn't mean your destiny has already been written. Self knowledge can go a long way toward freeing you from a certain behavior.

# Family Environment

*I don't want to give you the wrong impression. My dad never hit us. He carried a gun. If we did something wrong, we'd just hear "Click, Click."*

*My dad was the kind of dad who didn't like people. We'd be driving along the street and he'd spot someone who was a little different and he'd slow the car down. "Look at that. For crying out loud. Louie, get my rifle!"*

*My dad would say "shut up" a lot:*
*"Shut up! I'm trying to think."*
*"We could be here all month," I'd reply.*
*"Shut up!"*

**D**on't you wish you could adjust your family environment like the climate control system in your car? *Hmm, just let me turn down that family yelling a bit. Oh, and I think I'll turn up my dad's generous mood so I can get a bigger allowance.*

What was the weather report in *your* house? Chances

are, even if it was snowy *outside,* there were days when it was bright and sunny *inside*—when there was no fighting at breakfast, when they canceled school because of the blizzard and you shoveled the walk without being asked to and Dad even complimented you on the job you did.

On the other hand, there were probably days when it was beautiful outside, but partly cloudy inside. Mom might be so worried about Dad losing his job that she washed red with all the whites and you had to go to school in pink underwear and endure your brother's advertising it to the whole school.

Maybe you spent your entire childhood in search of safety from the approaching storm. In the Anderson house the weather was mostly warm with an uncertain chance of showers. Of course, if my dad started drinking, the forecast changed quickly. Then it was "dark skies with a tornado watch." I'm not saying we didn't have some really nice days, but the unpredictability definitely shaded our outlook. As the sun peeked through the rain clouds, we kids kept looking for rainbows.

The environment we grow up in greatly affects the extent to which we display our natural-born talents. If the climate is chaotic, a lot of energy is diverted to coping with the changes. If, on the other hand, life has a certain amount of predictability and stability and we receive positive reinforcement, those talents have a chance to blossom.

## FAMILY SURVIVAL TIP

### (for a change in the weather)

#19 What type of weather is typical for your household? Are most days beautiful with clear skies? Or is it the same turbulent family atmosphere you grew up in? Be wary of re-creating your childhood environment simply for the sake of familiarity. Force yourself to find the thermostat and keep adjusting.

# Family Placement

Location, location, location. Just as it's important in real estate, it's crucial in analyzing how you relate to your family. I'm sure it helped that I was second to the last in a large family. Many of the biggest family battles had already been fought, and several of my older brothers and sisters were gone from the nest by the time I showed up. My mother had time for me and she'd always make me feel special. We'd be making cookies in the kitchen and she'd whisper to me that I was the greatest and that there wasn't anything I couldn't do. (Little did I know that she was also doing that with the rest of my siblings.)

I was also lucky in that all my older brothers were out of the house and couldn't give me noogies like the ones I dispensed to my younger brother Mikey. Siblings tend to look for the spot that's open. Since criminal, crazy, and normal were already taken, I could shoot for wildly successful and famous.

I hear a lot of talk about sibling rivalry. I'm not sure how much of that existed in my family. At the Anderson homestead, we were just trying to survive. But I certainly have a lot of friends who've had to deal with this. To me, sibling rivalry is a question of resources. For example, seven puppies trying to get nourishment when there are only six teats. People look for a way to get attention. A famous model-actress who's made millions off her looks (and talent) once confessed to me that she never really felt pretty because growing up her older sister was always the one people described as "beautiful." Perhaps that was part of what drove her to become famous.

Family placement can be hard to shake. To this day, when I call my brother Frank, no matter what my situation, I'm conscious of his "older brother" status. No matter how many cable specials or Emmys I have, I'm still his *little* brother Louie. *He's* the one in charge; *he's* the one who picks the restaurant.

Of course, I'm not the only one with this problem. Look at the Bush family. Older brother George W. was the rebel; he spent more time having fun than doing his homework. Meanwhile, younger brother Jeb was Mr. Serious. He applied himself, always did the responsible thing. Then it comes time to run for president and who gets the shot? It's the ultimate older-brother noogie.

## FAMILY SURVIVAL TIP

### (for those unhappy with their location)

**#20 Family rank.** Just because you came out of the womb before or after your siblings doesn't mean it has to determine who you are. It is true, though, that birth order has a way of assigning "roles," and that you must be aware of the role you're unwittingly playing before you can initiate change. By the way, that George W. guy who never seemed to take things seriously eventually proved to himself and the world that just because you don't do your homework when you're a kid doesn't mean you can't get the job done later on.

# Family Storage

*My mom was a pack rat. She never threw anything out. Even garbage bags. After putting away the groceries, I'd sometimes make the mistake of attempting to throw the paper bag away only to hear my mom utter:*

*"What are you doing?"*

*"I'm throwing the bag away."*

*"Who do you think we are, the Rockefellers?"*

*"You want me to keep it?"*

*"I certainly do. That's a good bag."*

*"You want me to add it to that fire hazard you got goin' between the fridge and the cupboard? That salute to containers . . ."*

*My mom never missed an opportunity to pick up things she didn't need. For instance, at garage sales. She was always trying to get me to go in with her.*

*"Louie, come on. You might find a shirt that fits you."*

*"What, is Raymond Burr having a sale?"*

*We'd be there and she'd inevitably find something.*

*"Look, Louie, that toaster's only a quarter."*

*"It's broken."*

*"The cord alone is worth a quarter."*

*"Great. Next time I'm buying a soda, I'll throw four toaster cords down on the counter and see if they'll accept that."*

When it became necessary to move from Las Vegas to Los Angeles to begin hosting *The Feud*, I discovered something about myself. I owned a lot of stuff. Too much stuff. Even though I was moving into a pretty big house, it still wasn't large enough to fit all I had. So I was forced to put a lot in storage. Going through all my possessions triggered many family-related questions. For example: Why do we buy all this crap? What purpose does it serve?

I have all these Tiffany-style lamps. She could always spot a good one. "See that lamp, Louie. It gives off just the right light." *The right light.* What a great concept— that some light is better for seeing things clearly. Moms are always trying to be helpful like that: turning *on* lights when you're reading in the dark; turning *off* lights so the capacity of the nearby nuclear power plant isn't drained.

Mom, maybe if I find just the right light one day I won't need to collect all these lamps.

I know it isn't politically correct, but for a while, I had a huge collection of smoking paraphernalia. I told myself it was a way to get myself to quit smoking. Instead of buying cigarettes, I'd just buy expensive lighters and ashtrays. (By the way, it didn't work.) Maybe the smoking collection was in some way a tribute to my dad, who smoked his whole life. Or maybe it was just me thinking it was a good investment, since with everyone quitting smoking, there'd be less of this stuff around.

I also have a set of four paintings I picked up in a garage sale. They're all family portraits gone awry. They have these sad expressions on their greenish-tinted faces. What interested me about the paintings was that they captured this family in a state of seeming misery. I like to believe they were painted by an amateur artist who didn't know enough to lie about his subjects. For a while, I kept these portraits in my bedroom to remind myself that there existed at least one family more miserable than mine. I'd look up at their melancholy expressions and tell myself: *Hey, compared to them, I'm having a good day.*

I also own an enormous amount of furniture in a wide variety of styles—from expensive signed Stickley pieces to furniture made out of twigs. Stickley mission-style furniture was originally made by consummate craftsman Gustav Stickley who rebelled against the mass-produced furniture that became popular right before the turn of the twentieth century. He taught the business to his brothers, Leopold, Albert, John George, and Charles. The Stickleys believed in straightforward furniture—smooth lines, beautiful finishes, and no frills—leaving the precious Victorian style that preceded them behind. Of course, as all this handcrafting and meticulousness became less profitable, the brothers began to quarrel over just how much to deviate from their traditional ways. This being a *family* business, things got heated and the brothers all split off from Gustav and then each other.

It's perhaps not just a coincidence that a myth persists about the Stickley brothers helping to design an early version of the electric chair.

I've been thinking about the different furniture styles I've chosen and have decided each has been an attempt to create a home I never felt I had. *If I can get just the right chairs and sofa,* my unconscious mind says, *then maybe I can have that perfect home.* Currently, my house is full of fifties furniture, tastefully done. (Yes, fifties furniture *can* be tastefully done.) It's not lost on me that the

decade most identified with hominess is the fifties—
when families worked, at least on TV. The fifties are also
when I did a good part of my growing up. Maybe I'm
buying the furniture my mom and dad could never
afford.

*Look, guys, we have nice stuff. See, everything's okay.*

## FAMILY SURVIVAL TIP

### (for those pack rats in us all)

**#21 Family storage.** Look at the childhood possessions
you still cling to. What images are you trying to hold on
to from your past? Do these objects signify what really
was, or rather, what you *hoped*
for? Who decides what's
kept and thrown out in your
family? If you're someone who
doesn't keep anything, what are
you trying *not* to look at?

# Family Games

While putting my stuff in storage, I came across an old Rock 'Em Sock 'Em Robot set that I picked up as a kid and remember playing with with my brother Mikey. For those of you who never had one, this game featured two plastic robots trying to knock each other's heads off. A perfect game for brothers. A flaw in our set was that the blue robot's head was always broken and popped up easier, so I convinced Mikey that red was my favorite color and ended up creaming him every time.

Hey, don't feel too bad. Mikey would be "the bank" in Monopoly and just when I thought I had him beat, he'd conveniently find a few hundred bucks mysteriously hidden under the board, which he called his "reserve" money.

Cheating in family games is a rich tradition. How about Scrabble? People who play that game are always trying to use words that don't exist.

"Krisk."

" 'Krisk' isn't a word?!"

"Krisk! That's where Krisco comes from."

"Mom, there's no such word as 'krisk,' is there?"

"I'm not sure. Ask your father."

"Da-a-d—?!"

"Shut up or I'll come over there and kick you in the krisk."

"See, told ya."

Often, playing family games is just another way of getting your parents' attention.

Sometimes, it's not your parents' attention you seek but your siblings'. My friend Kurt spent years looking for an electric football set that he and his brother Tom used to play with when they were kids. Electric football involves a metal football field and tiny plastic players mounted on green brushes. The brushes magically move the men downfield when you turn on the switch, causing the whole field to vibrate. You line up teams against each other and, by ingenious positioning, try to get to your guy with the ball to penetrate the opposing team's defense and move forward toward the goal line. (For you younger folks, this is what we did before Nintendo and Xbox.)

Anyway, Kurt's wife bought him a new reproduction of the electric football game, but he returned it. It just wasn't the right one. He had to find one from 1975 and he had to find the right teams: Steelers against the Vikings. He had a score to settle. He became obsessed. Finally, after several bidding wars on eBay, he obtained the same version of the game he and his brother had played over twenty years earlier, complete with relatively unused puffy footballs that could be tucked into the arms of the plastic running back or flicked over the tiny plastic goal posts by the plastic kicker.

So Kurt invited Tom over to the house for their own private Super Bowl. No wives, no kids. Just mano a mano. They had a couple beers as they set up the game, both arguing about who'd won more when they played as kids. At first, Tom could barely remember even playing. But then as they started talking about it, he claimed Kurt never beat him—that he was undefeated. The discussion quickly degenerated into a debate over who'd been the better athlete, who'd gotten the cuter girls, which of the brothers their parents liked better. Finally, their machismo at a full boil, they lined up their men and after careful strategizing turned on the switch. The board vibrated and the little plastic men immediately headed toward the sidelines, where they remained jammed in place, out of action. Kurt and Tom both cracked up laughing. They suddenly remembered that the damned game they owned as kids never worked either. And at that moment, Kurt realized it was never about winning—it was about having a brother to play the game with.

## FAMILY SURVIVAL TIP

### (for the game players)

**#22 The games families play.** It seems to me that family games are a mostly healthy way of working out family issues. But watch how people play and you'll learn a lot about who your family members are. I have a friend whose father always defeated him at every game they played. Now a father himself, my friend lets his kids win. Did you come from a family where Dad let you beat him in checkers, or did he fight to the bitter end? Maybe answering that question will give you clues as to why, as an adult, you relate the way you do to your boss.

# Family Shopping

Sometimes I'll pull into a Wal-Mart late at night and it will be packed with families. I always wonder what people are looking for there. Do they *really* need more stuff? Or is there just something comforting about the shopping experience? There's a cell phone commercial that shows a family arriving at a mall, each equipped with a phone. They split up and happily conquer their shopping while keeping in touch via cell. "It's the new family plan," the commercial touts, unaware of its irony. In a way shopping has replaced the nightly ritual of family dinners. We don't have time to eat together—but, man, can we shop!

The implicit premise: Maybe if we buy Junior that G.I. Joe Jeep, or get ourselves that leather jacket we've been coveting, maybe then we'll be happy.

I know it sounds silly. But isn't that what we've been sold since we were first plunked down in front of a television set? *See that family on TV—the one where Dad just bought his daughter a new CD player (a CD player in her brand new Lexus)—that family is happy.* Gimme that Lexus and I'll be happy too. At least for a few minutes. Then comes the credit-card bills and the fighting and the what-have-you-got-*me*-lately looks and suddenly it's, *What can I get her/him next to make him/her happy?* It's a vicious cycle.

Loading up at the Gap is the new addiction. The desperate hope: If we fill our houses with stuff, maybe we won't have to deal with what's going on inside.

## FAMILY SURVIVAL TIP

### (for those who can't resist a sale)

**#23 Shopping: the new family dinner.** If shopping is the new family dinner in *your* family, make it as meaningful as possible. Realize this is how you're spending time with your loved ones and don't let the things you're buying get in the way of connecting with each other. Even better, instead of spending all that extra time working to buy things for your family, try allocating it to actually *being* with your family. See if they (and you) don't enjoy that more.

# Family Feud #1

## (everything in life can be learned from game shows)

It's ironic that I would end up hosting *Family Feud* for three years. If I ever imagined hosting a game show, it was probably something like *Family Food.* When the offer came, I called my best friend—a man who cares more about my spiritual well-being than my career in show business—and asked what he thought. "Well, Louie," he reminded, "you do stand-up comedy about your *family*, you wrote a book about your *family*, you created a cartoon about your *family*, you're making a documentary about your *family*. And nobody would know more about feuding with your *family* . . ."

Thank God for best friends.

Doing *The Feud* turned out to be a great experience, helping me more than I expected to learn what families truly are and how they affect us. Part of the show's appeal, I believe, is that, in contrast to questions that come up with most families, the questions on the show are easily answered. Well, by some anyway.

I still laugh at the woman who, when asked to name a way to prepare chicken, answered, "Thawed out." Then there was the contestant who, when asked to name a famous George, answered "Steely George." When I asked what he meant, he said, "You know, that band 'Steely George.'" "You mean, Steely *Dan*?" From that moment on, I knew his family nickname would be "Steely George." Hey, there's a lot of pressure when you're answering those questions on TV.

Of course, there's also the theory that by the time you select *five* family members for the show . . . Well, let's face it, pick five members from *any* family. Okay, *you're* smart, but go a few people down the line and you're bound to find a light bulb that doesn't shine too bright.

One of the perks of hosting *The Feud* was all the families I got to meet. Because I was giving away money (or at least *trying*—I really did want them to win that $20,000), I wasn't allowed to interact with them before the show. But I enjoyed watching the wide variety of family dynamics.

Take, for example, the way a family's designated

spokesman introduces his fellow members. *This is my wacky cousin Shirley, this is my handsome brother Donald, this is my brilliant uncle Fred.* The show's producers ask contestants to boil down descriptions to a few words, but when you think about it, that's fitting. Family members *do* tend to label each other with a few words.

Of course, just because you're known as the "wacky cousin" doesn't mean you have to live up to the label. You *can* redefine yourself. Just because you've been an underachiever in the past, doesn't mean you have to mess up the job you have now. Just because you were always the responsible one doesn't mean you can't have fun and cut loose every once in a while.

Sometimes I wonder how people would introduce their families if they weren't on television:

"This is my cousin Stacy. She's a very friendly girl— a little *too* friendly if you know what I mean."

"This is my uncle Phil. His workaholic ways resulted in my cousin Stacy's not getting enough attention as a kid, so she now sleeps around."

"This is my aunt Sara. She was hypercritical of my uncle Phil, which caused him to spend all the time at the office, which of course caused my cousin Stacy to become promiscuous."

"And let's not forget Grandma Doris who constantly berated Aunt Sara about every aspect of her behavior, which caused her to develop an anal personality, which, in turn, led to her hypercriticism."

Of course, I'm sure these descriptions don't match any family *you* know.

## FAMILY SURVIVAL TIP

### (for the contestant in all of us)

**#24 Family introductions.** How would you introduce your family on *The Feud*? How would your family introduce you? If you like what you hear, fine. But remember, you don't have to be that. And be careful not to label other family members. A friend recently told me about his early years as a struggling actor trying to make it in New York theater. He was broke, one step away from homelessness, when his teenage brother, the black sheep of the family who back then was supporting himself selling pot, showed up and offered to make his rent payment. It was a simple, kind gesture and exactly what my friend needed at the time. Sometimes, help can come from the most unlikely places—even from a family member everyone has voted "*least* likely to."

# Family Feud #2

## (it's not just a TV show)

I'm up onstage in Syracuse, New York, when an audience member calls out "How's your brother Mikey?" He mimics a bullying gesture I use in my act when I'm teasing my younger brother. It never fails to get applause. I was born with five brothers and five sisters, but eight-year-old Louie's teasing six-year-old Mikey has been a crowd pleasure since I first did *The Tonight Show.* Mikey even inspired the title of one of my first cable specials, *Mom! Louie's Looking at Me Again!*

*It's fun having younger brothers. You don't have to hit them. You just get up in the morning and look at them across the breakfast table.*

*You know the look—you scrunch up your face, bug out your eyes, and stick out your tongue.*

*You do that look long enough and you'll hear this every time:*

*"Mo-o-m-m-m, Louie's looking at me again!"*

*Then I go into my older brother defense:*

*"What, is it against the law to look at people? Look, Ma, does this face bother you?"*

*I give her that sweet, innocent-Louie, total-angel-boy look no mother can resist.*

*She turns to my brother. "Mikey, stop it."*

*"What did I do?"*

*After breakfast, Mikey and I would have to go clean our room. Of course, since I was older, I was in charge:*

*"This area I'm standing in, that's the area I'll be cleaning. The rest of this filthy pigpen is yours. Oh, yeah, by the way, Mom told me to tell you this today . . . you're adopted."*

*"I am not!"*

*"They were frog-faced people—I saw them drop you off. They had eyes that bugged out of their heads. And they told me that when you turn thirteen, your eyes are going to pop out. The only cure is to tape your eyes down with this masking tape . . ."*

*The fun part was the next morning when Mom would come into our room and look at Mikey laying there asleep with tape over his eyes and ask in her quiet, gentle way: "What the heck is going on here?"*

*I'd look at her innocently, the concerned older sibling. "I think he's on dope, Mother."*

*She'd go over and rip the tape off his eyes. He'd wake up screaming and try to explain things, but in that blubbering voice, "Lou . . . ee . . . said . . . that . . . I'm . . ."*

*Before he could reveal what was going on, my mom would shake him and ask: "Are you on drugs?!"*

Mikey, the forever picked on younger brother. To be fair, I also talk about how my four older brothers used to torment *me* in my gullible years.

*"Louie, see that swamp over there?" one of my older brothers would ask.*

*"Yeah?"*

*"There's a monster in it."*

*"There is? Well, it's a good thing we're over here then."*

*"You know, its arms could reach over here if it wanted to . . ."*

*After that, for years I'd walk way out of my way of avoid the swamp. That is, until I got a little older, a little smarter, and a little brother . . .*

*"Mikey, you see that swamp over there? That's where your* real *parents live."*

Audiences always love when I joke about torturing Mikey. They know it's all in fun. About a year ago, I exited the stage to find my assistant Raul waiting with phone in hand and a sad expression. He told me to call my sister Tina. Something was up with Mikey. This of course wasn't six-year-old Mikey, but forty-six-year-old Mikey. But does age really make a difference when it comes to family?

Months before, my brother Mikey had been living in Las Vegas and I'd encouraged him to come to California where I now live so I could set him up in his own apartment. I thought L.A. would be a better environment for him and was looking forward to his being closer. He'd seemed lost ever since my mom's death.

This night I was performing, though, Tina told me she and Mikey had a fight and that Mikey had taken off for the streets. You're never too old to run away from home. I would've put out an A.P.B. on him, but he bears a remarkable resemblance to myself. With my luck, *I'd* get picked up.

Jokes aside, I was worried.

# raternal

I could tell you the simple story. The one you see on those movies of the week where one brother goes and rescues the other. It usually works best if the younger brother has some disease he can't help getting, like autism or Tourette's, which causes him to swear at all the social workers. The older brother quits his job and spends all this time with the younger brother until he's cured and can live on his own without cussing.

Oh, if it were that easy. I'd like to paint myself as a hero, and the truth is, I'd do anything to help Mikey. But somehow it got more complicated.

A few weeks later, things had settled down somewhat and I told Mikey I wanted to see him at four o'clock on Saturday. Meanwhile, he directed angry outbursts at my sister Tina. (Large families, particularly mine, are like the guys on the old *Ed Sullivan Show* who had to spin all those plates at the same time. Every time you think you're doing all right over on one side, you have to rush over and grab the plate that's about to fall on the other.)

Apparently, Mikey was jealous because I'd let my sister and her miniature Doberman pinscher Duchess live at my house. I had no choice—Duchess would have nipped at my ankles till I agreed. But Mikey never *said* he was jealous. Instead, he acted out, screaming at Tina, calling her "the mole" as she dropped him off somewhere. There are worse things to call people than a mole. I'm not even really sure I know what that means. It's not *what* you say in families, but the *way* you say them.

In sitcoms, family members always have these witty retorts ready. Show a *real* family in action—well, most real families I know—and it would make *COPS* seem like a Disney special. At least, if you catch the family at certain moments.

Back to Mikey. I was so pissed at the way he was treating Tina that I wrote him a note telling him I appreciated the rough childhood we all went through, but that there was no way I could see him given the way he was acting toward people.

*Dear Mikey,*

    *Sorry we couldn't meet Wednesday, but I didn't get home until 10:30 P.M. because I was so tired I was able to get the* Nash Bridges *people [I'd just filmed a guest spot] to let me come up on a later flight.*

    *I asked Tina to give you a message about meeting Saturday, but after what you said to Raul [my assistant], I felt I should write this letter. There's no excuse to say those kinds of things to Raul or anyone else. It hurt me and you were mean to say them. It makes me never want to see you. Everyone tries to help you, but you don't care or it's never enough. Well, I'm sick of it.*

    *There is a reason you are getting disability from Social Security right now. It's because you, like all of us in the family, have problems. No one cares more about you than I do, but if you won't help yourself or get some kind of help, there's nothing anyone can do.*

*When you decide to get some help or need some assistance with this, I will meet with you and try to help. But I'm not your mom and you constantly hurt me and others. People love you and if you want them to care, you can't keep hurting them.*

*Mikey, why do you feel you should be taken care of? No one takes care of me. I know things can be rough, that's why I go to therapy. I will talk to you about any of this, but not if you continue to hurt me and others. Maybe you think I've tried to hurt you, but I haven't and if I have hurt your feelings, it was not my intent.*

*I know things that happened to you growing up were horrible, but things happened to me too. That's why I got some help. I love you.*

> Your brother,
> Louie

I was pleased with myself, thinking I'd expressed myself clearly and that my tough love had made its point. Saturday came and Mikey called at 1:30 P.M. With absolutely no acknowledgment of having received my letter, he told me he'd be ready and waiting for me to pick him up at 3:30. Not even 4:00, when I'd originally told him I'd meet him. Only a brother, a younger brother, would even *try* to get away with stuff like this.

I had a good notion to blow off getting together with him completely. I really wanted to go to Las Vegas anyway where I could forget about everything but the cards being dealt by the video poker machine. But I'd closed my checking account and only had one small credit line set up. (Previously I'd been told by someone from one of the hotels who keeps track of this stuff that they rate gamblers on a one to ten scale, one being oil tycoons who gamble a million a hand. At one point, I

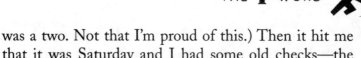

was a two. Not that I'm proud of this.) Then it hit me that it was Saturday and I had some old checks—the casinos wouldn't know my account was closed. (I'd told myself I wasn't going to do this anymore.)

And then my thoughts drifted back to Mikey. Maybe in his present state, this was as close as he could get to saying he was sorry. I love him so I decided to keep the meeting, but I wasn't going to take any crap. Then a strange, insane thought occurred to me. Maybe he was planning on killing me.

Oh, yeah, it seems crazy, but isn't every other *Dateline* these days about some family member killing another? And the juries are always ready to believe the family member did it. They know how families are. "Hey, who *hasn't* thought about killing his wife?" the jury foreman told Stone Phillips on the episode I'd watched a week before. A cop at the Grand Canyon once told me that every year, particularly during black ice season when you can't see where it's slippery, one or two people intentionally push their spouses off the edge into the canyon. (Please note: This is *not* a family survival tip.)

Like all Andersons, Mikey is a big guy and, at times, can seem dangerous and unstable. Growing up, I could always take him. But as the years passed I got the feeling he thought he could take *me*. Didn't he know about the unwritten rule that states older brothers are *always* supposed to be able to beat up younger ones?

That Saturday Mikey could have been carrying a knife or a club or a sharp potato peeler. But what the hell, if he killed me, he killed me. I believe in destiny and seat belts.

Driving through the rain, I headed into the valley and turned onto Mikey's street. There he was, nearly a carbon copy of myself. As I watched him pace back and forth, I wondered whom he'd be waiting for if I'd never become a success and moved him and our brother Bill to L.A. from Vegas. Bill is a true paranoid schizophrenic who wandered the West for almost twenty years with very few contacts. Except during his two-year prison stint, we really never knew where he was. He always thought he was being followed, and believed he'd been abducted by aliens. Who knows—maybe all of us Andersons are aliens. That would certainly explain things.

Sometimes I wonder if Mikey's living with Bill for several years caused him to catch Bill's sickness. Is mental illness contagious?

The second I saw Mikey close up I knew he was having a good day. He gave me the customary Anderson hug-and-kiss greeting. Such intimacy for a family that has always struggled with intimacy. I asked him if he wanted to do something spontaneous and go to Vegas for the night. He lit up a cigarette and said, "Sure." I inquired if he needed anything from his apartment before we left. He laughed and said no, he didn't have *anything*—a not-so-subtle dig at my status as celebrity brother who supposedly has *everything*.

At this point, I should confess that I had a small bag already packed in the trunk. My plan had been to head to the airport after this get-together and catch a plane to Vegas for some of my version of R&R. But standing there in front of Mikey, I kept getting the sense that there was something he was trying to express. Maybe it was as simple as *Hey, Lou, I want to spend some time with you.*

What my family doesn't realize is that basically I'm a loner and because I felt some resentment toward them at the time, I didn't always want to share their company. Ugly thoughts, I know.

As we pulled out of the driveway, Mikey mentioned that he hadn't been sure we were still meeting, that he'd been going to reread my note but had thrown it in the trash. I couldn't help pick up a subconscious dig there— that in *his* mind what I have to say is trash. I almost said something to him, but resisted, using my patented "count-to-five" system. I know it's supposed to be count-to-ten, but I never have the patience to make it that far.

We gassed up, got some drinks, Mikey nabbed some muffins, and we headed to Vegas. Mikey is always saying that the stuff between us has nothing to do with money. I couldn't help thinking about this as I paid for his beverages and cigarettes. People think that because you have money you should pay for *everything*. Even friends of mine who make a good living are slow to pull out their wallets when I'm around. Sometimes I'll go to the bathroom when the check arrives just to see if they're going to pick it up.

I admit, it's hard to pick up a check around me. But come on, people. Once in a while, show some character. If you're going to be cheap with money, you're going to be cheap with everything, including friendship.

As Mikey and I drove toward the desert, I felt like maybe this would work out. Then he reached into his jacket and I flinched for a second, for some reason fantasizing he was about to pull out a knife or a gun. Instead, it was only cigarettes.

Of course, cigarettes kill people too. My brother Kyle is suffering from emphysema and I myself have been trying to quit for years. I tried the patch, but decided I need a nicotine jacket. I've saved up enough of those Marlboro points that I almost have enough to buy a respirator. Two hundred more packs and I'll have enough for that really nice coffin they offer.

Many of us Andersons smoke. As Mikey lit up, I thought about offering everyone in my family a new car if they'd quit. There I was again, believing I could change people. Hey, I smoke as much as any of them. Maybe I should buy *myself* a new car if I quit.

The thing about driving from L.A. to Vegas is, it's close enough to talk yourself into driving, but after about an hour in the car, you get bored and start berating yourself for not just taking the half-hour flight. All you have to look forward to is three more hours of looking at desert. I kept thinking about how I was going to broach the subject of what Mikey was going to do with his life. But he didn't seem to be leaving any openings. I was about to launch into a lecture when I thought about my own mental condition and realized I needed to take it slow, just offer my love and support. Hell, we might even end up becoming friends.

We arrived about 8:30 P.M., checked into the Venetian, and I set out to break the bank. Or at least to get lost in the soothing blue screen of the video poker machine. I cashed a check and gave Mikey some money, wondering if this gesture would send the wrong message. I liked to play the high-limit machines and was a bit surprised when Mikey put one of the hundred-dollar bills I gave him into the high-roller machine next to me. Calculating that the thousand bucks I gave him would be gone in ten minutes, I told him he'd make his money last longer if he played cheaper stakes. Then I found myself amending the comment and telling him to play whatever he wanted. I needed to stop acting like a parent and behave more like a friend. Plus, I reminded myself, he hadn't *asked* for the money.

The truth is, I don't like anyone sitting next to me when I play the machines. I like to focus on playing and don't want to be distracted. I was torn. I was here to be with Mikey. But sometimes I just don't like people around. I know I'm too sensitive, but the littlest thing can set me off. It was then I realized I'd brought along some Vicodin pills. They'd help get rid of the edginess.

It was ironic that I wanted Mikey to seek help from a professional, who'd probably balance his mood swings with medication. And here I was, relying on a substance that would help me do the same.

Just as I thought, ten minutes later Mikey was out of money. I gave him another five hundred and again suggested he try cheaper machines. He reluctantly moved off and I was relieved. But why? What kind of relationship with Mikey did I really want? How could I help my family members when I myself had so many problems?

Months later, things were looking up. Mikey's situation was much improved. Was it due to my love and support, his effort and determination, or his courage in seeking out mental-health professionals? Regardless, the important thing is he's making progress toward a more stable, happy, and productive life. And hopefully, I can say the same about myself.

## FAMILY SURVIVAL TIPS
### (for those with siblings)

**#25 All in the same boat.** When we set out from home, leaving our families behind, we head like explorers down the Amazon, negotiating treacherous rapids, overcoming obstacles, experiencing setbacks. We think we're the only ones who've ever been through these parts. But guess what? We often discover that our siblings are in the same boat.

**#26 Six or forty-six.** In the new life we've created for ourselves we may be mountain climbers, CEOs, or neurosurgeons. But around siblings, we frequently regress to the people we were when we were kids. Just concede that you're still going to make a certain amount of faces at each other across the breakfast table.

**#27 Lower expectations.** You may think you're going to change a family member, but change is never easy. In the movie *Rain Main* an emotionally closed-off Tom Cruise discovers he has a brother Raymond, played by Dustin Hoffman. Raymond is autistic, but still, Cruise's character is convinced he can get through to him. In the end, it's Cruise who changes. Maybe Raymond loves him an inch more—which is as far as he can go for who he is. But Cruise actually takes off his cool sunglasses for a moment and tells Raymond he cares about him. (Then, of course, the sunglasses go right back on.) We all relate to that movie because it's true. Autistic or not, people change in inches, not yards.

# Fantasy Family

*The Godfather* is such a powerful movie because it's not really about the Mafia, but about family. Backstabbing partners, conniving thieves, ruthless murderers—no wonder it reminds everyone of their family (minus the guns and racketeering). Come to think of it, we Andersons had that too.

Spending time with your family makes you think of how you'd *like* them to be. You know how in fantasy baseball you get to pick your players from anyone in the Major Leagues? What if we had a chance to pick our relatives? Who would *you* go with? When I was growing up, we all wanted to be one of the Cleavers, the Waltons or the Bradys. Unfortunately, our real families were more like the Bundys, the Simpsons, or even the Mansons.

My friend Simon grew up with a single mom and he remembers as a kid watching *The Mary Tyler Moore Show* alone on Saturday night while his mom was on dates. To him, Mary was like his mother, trying to make it on her own. Mary's friends, Mr. Grant, Murray, Ted, and Georgette, were the family he longed for. They were always there for each other, and at the end of each episode everything turned out all right. Simon also devotedly watched *The Brady Bunch,* but the woman his father had remarried was nothing like Carol Brady. Carol would never have ordered her stepson to stand in the corner for "sassing" while yelling at him that he should act more like those Brady kids on TV.

Every sitcom, whether it's *Gilligan's Island, Family Ties,* or *Friends,* provides the fantasy family we'd all like to have—people who care about each other and can work out whatever problems exist within thirty minutes. Where the sitcoms actually reflect reality is that the same problems tend to emerge week after week. Usually, the Michael J. Fox character ends up in the kitchen apologizing for being overly concerned with money and disregarding his family.

The TV family I most identified with was the one in *All in the Family.* Archie was my frustrating but lovable and oh-so-wrong dad. Even when I couldn't find love for my dad, I could always find warm feelings for Carroll O'Connor. And who was *I* in this fantasy family? Meathead, of course. Eating all of Archie's food while telling him how wrong he was. In the seventies I think a lot of kids felt that way toward their parents.

The other day someone came up to me and told me how much they'd enjoyed my cartoon *Life with Louie* and what a great family I had. That show was my chance to re-create my family with the flaws taken out. Instead of being an alcoholic, my dad was just a beloved grump. And he was always there to solve problems—at least, trying to, until Mom came in to save the day. It was very healing for me to live in that universe for the few years I was working on the show. We should all get a chance to create a world where everything works out. It lets us know what to shoot for.

In *Life with Louie*, my dad coached my softball team, took Little Louie hunting (where they eventually did *not* kill the deer), and helped Louie out when he plagiarized an essay in order to win a trip to Washington. Dad did everything I always wanted him to do. *Of course*, he did. After all, not only was I the producer of the show, but I did both my father's and Little Louie's voice. In reality, my father was more disappointing than helpful. But by creating these episodes, I got in touch with the things I'd longed for. And now, when family situations arise, I try to be the supportive guy my fictional dad was. Who doesn't want to be the hero in the end?

## FAMILY SURVIVAL TIP

### (for the family we all longed for)

**#28 Create your own fantasy family.** Imagine what you'd like your family to be like. How would your fantasy family handle situations your real family now has trouble with? Try to coax your real family into being the fantasy family for a day and see what happens. (WARNING: Mike Brady speeches have limited effect when talking with your kids about gang violence and crack. And avoid lines like "You know, when I was growing up, Bobby . . .")

# Family-isms

Later in life, my father developed Parkinson's disease, which caused him to shake sometimes. At least, that's what the doctors told us. My mother, observing the symptoms, said the shaking was due to my father's having once worked with jackhammers.

Dad's analysis of symptoms could be equally curious. He believed he had ingrown toenails because he was forced to wear shoes that were too tight.

Recently, I met someone who doesn't answer her phone during thunderstorms because her mother told her you can get electrocuted through the phone line during a lightning storm. (Hey, that one could even be right!)

Someone else's family learned their mother had cancer, but ten years have passed and they still haven't told her. They're convinced "not telling her" is keeping her alive.

A friend of mine has a two-year-old daughter and a wife who keeps yelling at him to put down the toilet seat. Her scolding comment: "Do you have any idea how many kids drown in toilets each year?" (As far as I know, zero.)

## FAMILY SURVIVAL TIP

### (for separating family truth from falsehood)

**#29 Get a second opinion.** Family members who think they're doctors would have you believe that if you listen to music too loud you'll go deaf, if you run with a scissors you'll lose an eye, and if you eat and go swimming without waiting an hour, you'll get a cramp and die. Family wisdom also holds that you'll go blind by reading in the dark, sitting too close to the TV, or pleasuring yourself in the bathroom. It's amazing the entire country isn't wearing glasses. The point of all these examples: Question the folklore that gets passed down to you.

# Family ABCs

One of my neighbors is always spelling things rong—wrong. When she was a kid, she learned how to read by something called the "whole word" method instead of phonetically. This woman goes through her days continually asking people how to spell because of the way she was initially taught.

What other things do we learn incorrectly early on? How about how to deal with frustration, money, competition, drugs, sex, and love? I always wondered why they make kids take all these classes in geometry, Spanish, and social studies, but there's not one course on how to handle emotions. Isn't that important—particularly today, when students have to cope with events like school shootings? When I was growing up, the big worry was getting in trouble for chewing gum.

In his book *Emotional Intelligence,* Daniel Goleman talks about a straight-A student who knifed his physics teacher because he got a B on a test and was afraid he wouldn't get into Harvard medical school. Goleman's point is that having a high I.Q. doesn't make you brilliant at dealing with emotions—or, for that matter, dealing with your family.

Nonetheless, I always regretted that I didn't stick with formal education and go to college. It just wasn't emphasized in my upbringing. And truthfully, I always sensed I was smarter than my teachers. What I learned in school was: You can't teach an Anderson anything. That's because we already know everything.

Just ask my dad, who had a theory on the whole world, especially when he was drinking:

*"Louie! Life!! Live it!"*

Or my mom, who could have solved the Middle East conflict in a second.

*"The problem is that they have no hot water over there—you know, because it's a desert. What they all need is a good, long soak in the tub. After that, everyone feels a lot friendlier."*

Recently, I was asked to speak to a class of students at the University of Pittsburgh. I don't get nervous performing live in front of five thousand people or before a TV audience of millions. But I practically had to be pushed into this towering gothic structure, which was aptly named the Cathedral of Learning, to speak to twenty undergraduates. Once the class started up, though, I found the discussion invigorating. I was also touched to hear how many of the students had grown up watching *Life with Louie*. Okay, that made me feel a little *old*, but touched.

It's actually quite common for performers to be self-educated. Neither Tom Hanks nor Steven Spielberg (who was rejected by several film schools) were great students. Yet through their creative endeavors, they're now teaching the world about subjects like World War II and the space program. But what I realized from going to class that day was what I'd always suspected: I would have benefited a lot from going to college.

I didn't pursue a college degree because of what I was taught at home. It wasn't that anyone ever said "Hey, don't go to school." It was that no one made getting a sheepskin a priority. My mom was an avid reader and my dad always kept up with what was going on in the world. And that Anderson curiosity got passed down. I can't even *start* to go to sleep without reading a book (or at least listening to one on tape—my preferred method of reading).

Andersons tell their stories orally. To this day, I write all my comedy routines in my head. A book like this is a challenge because my upbringing never prepared me to be a writer in this way. I missed out on a lot because I didn't get how important education was when I was growing up. But it's never too late.

## FAMILY SURVIVAL TIPS
### (for the education we all need)

#30 We're all home-schooled. Once we realize what we learned wrong in our childhoods, we can re-teach ourselves how to do things. And we should also be aware of *why* we learned things wrong. The fact is, parents learn on the job and often make things up as they go along. So if you received incomplete or flawed lessons in basic math, anger management, nutritional eating, or how to have a decent relationship, it may be time to go back to kindergarten.

**#31 You can never cut the grass as good as your father.** Not that I *wanted* to cut it in the first place, but no matter what I did, my dad would come out and show me how it was done. Parents need to feel important, and well, heck, if they can't cut grass better than their kids, what *can* they teach them? Of course, now that I'm an adult I have my own gardeners. And guess what? I'm always out there showing them how they should do things. They never seem to get it right.

**#32 Our parents are only human.** Salman Rushdie wrote a brilliant essay on *The Wizard of Oz* in which he said that the movie is really about how ineffectual parents are. He said the Wizard, like the rest of the adults in the piece, is a bungling fool who can't get the job done. So it's left to Dorothy, the kid, to kill the wicked witch. It does seem to me that our dads greatly resemble that blustery old Wizard. They appear to be all-powerful, but when the curtain is pulled back, they're revealed as ordinary human beings. (Maybe our moms are the good witches—at least, in some cases.) In the end, the moral of *The Wizard of Oz* is that the power lies within us. It's important to remember that as we travel down the yellow brick road, coping with life. Our parents are only human.

# Fact. Fiction. Fantasy.

*You know how, when you went driving with your dad, he'd point out certain stuff to you:*

*"You see that bridge, Louie? I guarded it against the Germans in World War II."*

*"I never knew the Germans got to Minneapolis."*

*"You see that barrel factory?"*

*"Yeah."*

*"Look at it! I broke my ass there for fifty cents an hour so you kids could eat."*

*I never really knew what to say to this. I mean, I was two when he worked there.*

*"Thanks, Dad."*

*"And those Goddamn barrels were heavy!"*

*Then we'd drive on over to the dump.*

*"Hey, look. That chair. Not bad."*

*"Oh my God. We're shopping."*

*"You put a little duct tape on those cushions and you got yourself a real nice La-Z-Boy."*

*My dad was real proud of having gotten that chair at the dump. We'd have company over and he'd talk about it.*

*"Hey, you know I got this chair at the dump?"*

*Our guests would look down at the couch they were sitting on.*

*"Oh, really. And where did you get this . . . ?"*

*Maybe that was his way of making sure they didn't stay long.*

**M**y friend Fred was always telling me how he used to get beat up regularly at the playground when he was in elementary school. He's a successful adult now and has told the story amusingly for years about how the bullies at school would whitewash his face in the snow. Recently, for employment reasons, Fred moved back to his old hometown where these traumatic events occurred. By coincidence, the house he rented overlooked that old playground by his elementary school. And a funny thing happened as he walked back over the grounds where the alleged crimes had been committed.

Standing on the grassy area, which was much smaller than he'd remembered, he was suddenly unsure that his face really *had* been washed with snow. If the incidents had actually happened as he'd been telling everyone, wouldn't he have remembered the cold snow on his face? And that big hill he was supposed to have run up in his attempt to escape was hardly a hill at all. Thinking back on it, he wasn't even positive there *were* bullies. Well, maybe *once* someone had threatened to whitewash his face.

Where had this story about being beaten up regularly come from, he wondered? And why was he walking around with these ingrained memories?

What happened, the story we tell ourselves about what happened, and what we would like to have happened: fact . . . fiction . . . fantasy.

The problem is, it can get to the point where we can't tell the difference. Take my friend who used to get beat up. Or *thought* he had. He was probably traumatized by something on that playground. As a small boy, he felt unprotected from his tormentors. Perhaps the stories he told years later of having his face whitewashed were a kind of declaration—to himself and everyone else—that

he survived the experience. Perhaps his stories grew out
of a fantasy of wanting someone to have stepped in and
helped.

In the end, the person who helped him was himself:
By turning his frightened feelings into a story, the bullies—if they ever did exist—became mere characters in
a fiction.

This is a phenomenon I'm well acquainted with,
having made a nice living on the stories of my childhood. At this point, it's hard to sort through what's real
and what's made up. My dad never really carried a gun.
My mom didn't actually order butter while waiting for a
table. Those are pretty easy. There really *was* a dump—
the Pig's-Eye Dump, which was run by Native Americans who'd sort through people's trash and sell it in
garage-sale fashion. My dad would give them a couple
of bucks for the good stuff, including his favorite chair.
He really did work at a barrel factory, but he probably
made two fifty an hour, not fifty cents, worked six hours
a day instead of sixteen like he told us, and those barrels
he said weighed fifty pounds were probably empty. As
for guarding the bridge, well I believe he did do that.
During World War II, people had to guard shipments
that could be valuable. And it's true that, thanks to him,
the Germans never invaded the Twin Cities.

Basically, like many comedians I tell these stories to
point out their absurdity but also to state what we've all
experienced. The message is: Look at how goofy our
parents are. Because I'm standing there onstage, people
know I've survived. They're thinking: *Even if his dad did
threaten him with a gun, there he is. And his dad probably
didn't do that anyway—he's just having fun.*

Of course, at some level, I feel like my dad really *did*
do that.

As long as I'm going on record about this, I should add that many of the witty retorts I credit myself with in my act did not occur. Like when my dad said, "We didn't have school back when I was a kid. We had to find smart people and follow them around," and I shot back, "Bet you never found someone." That's clearly made up on *both* ends.

The interesting question is: Why? And the answer is: By inventing this fiction, I can rescript what actually happened. I may not have stood up to my dad then, but I do now—every time I tell that story.

In my childhood, as in many people's childhoods, Dad would often come up with the fiction, Mom would state the facts, and I'd supply the fantasy as a coping mechanism for what was going on. For instance, after a family get-together Dad would yell about what a witch Aunt Martha was and how she was always telling him what to do. My mother, the truth-teller, would remind him that he provoked her by getting drunk and mentioning she looked like a bearded monkey. And I'd just remember the great model airplane Aunt Martha got me as a present. I came up with this pleasant fantasy, like we all do, so I wouldn't have to deal with the ugly reality, which at the time I couldn't handle.

To sort out for myself what's fact, fiction, and fantasy, I thought I'd take a close look at an episode of *Life with Louie*. On our Thanksgiving show, Little Louie is forced to play a turkey in the school play, though he doesn't want to because he always gets "gobbled at" by the rest of the kids. Sure enough, the teacher forces him to anyway and after a few gobbles, an angry Louie dives into the audience, taking a few kids out with him. As punishment, he's made to do a report on the meaning of Thanksgiving.

Louie first seeks answers from his mother, who tells him that Thanksgiving is all about pumpkin pie—that during Thanksgiving the crust and the pumpkin filling come together to produce something magical. Louie's father then tells him that Thanksgiving is all about carving the turkey. Neither parent is much help.

But then during Thanksgiving, the rich uncle whom Louie's dad hates comes over, flying in on his private plane. The uncle steals all the attention, offering plane rides and engaging Dad in one-upmanship every chance he gets. The uncle claims he should carve the turkey because his family lineage can be traced back to the Pilgrims. Louie's dad counters by mentioning that *his* ancestors were at the real first Thanksgiving when Viking Gunther Anderson discovered America, pre-Miles Standish. Eventually, this leads to a wrestling match over the turkey that results in food spraying everywhere. As Louie dives to save a falling pumpkin pie and is nearly knocked unconscious, the uncle and dad realize how silly they've been. Mom points out to Dad that the real reason the uncle shows off is that he's jealous. You see, he has no family of his own. In the end, Louie does his report and his dad and uncle take off for a ride in the plane together.

A sweet little story, right? Only in the cartoons. But the facts are closer than you might think. I really did have a rich uncle Ike who actually owned a private plane that he used to fly from South Dakota to our place for the holidays. It's also true that Uncle Ike and his wife couldn't have any children of their own. Oh, and my dad really did hate him. One time, they actually got in a physical fight where my dad decked him.

The fiction my dad created was that Uncle Ike was

this horrible, selfish rich guy who could have helped them out, but chose not to. The fact that my mother would later reveal was that Uncle Ike *had* helped us out by helping us buy our first house—actually a duplex—and that my dad lost the place because he couldn't keep up the payments.

I couldn't accept that my dad was such a screwup, so I came up with this story—possibly a fantasy—that Uncle Ike never gave my dad enough money and that my dad didn't really want to take the money and that's why he self-destructed. I also found a way to see my dad as more successful than Uncle Ike in the long run because, though he didn't have material wealth, he had a whole family of kids who still talk about him to this day.

Some of this fantasy is helpful, but some of it obscures in a way that *isn't* helpful. Now that I'm an adult, I can see more dimensions to all the players. In trying to get at the heart of what was going on between Uncle Ike and Dad, I did some investigation and discovered the real reason for that physical fight between them. My sister Sally told me that when she was forty, our mother revealed to her an incident in which Uncle Ike and his wife went on a drive with my mom and dad. At the time, Sally and my sister Mary were living at my uncle's because of our family's hard times. My uncle Ike apparently suggested to my dad that he adopt the two girls. Though my dad had eleven kids and lacked the means to support them, Louie Sr. would hear none of it. Apparently, he blew up. (The physical fight might have occurred later after my dad was drinking.)

To my dad, the idea of someone else's adopting his kids, even my mother's sister and her husband, was unthinkable. He had too much pride to let something like that happen. It meant he was a failure. And coming from a boyhood where he'd been forced to live with foster parents, the notion of having to give up his own kids must have been extremely hurtful. Of course, my dad never told me any of this. Once again, it was Mom who got the facts out.

## FAMILY SURVIVAL TIP

### (for those with imagination)

**#33 Fact, fantasy, fiction.** I mentioned this idea of fact, fiction, and fantasy to my friend Debbie who was about to go out to dinner with her seventy-year-old father and ninety-three-year-old grandmother. When she was growing up, her father had always claimed to have never gone out to a restaurant in his whole childhood. That night Debbie brought up her dad's claim in front of her grandmother. Her grandmother immediately scoffed and began listing the number of restaurants he'd gone to as a kid. Debbie's father sheepishly admitted he'd gone to those places. Then why had he perpetuated this fiction? Did he for some reason need to feel deprived about his childhood? Later, Debbie guessed that her father had been uncomfortable spending money on restaurants when funds were tight, and created his restaurant-deprivation fantasy so he'd feel less guilty about not taking his kids out to eat. Of course, this may have been Debbie's fantasy about why her dad had created this fiction.

Go through the stories of your childhood and spot those that seem suspiciously like fiction. Try to get to the bottom of the reality that lies beneath, and ask yourself if there's a fantasy that connects the two. An acquaintance of mine, Steve, told me his mother never revealed the circumstances behind his parents' divorce until years later. He had no idea what had happened to his dad so he fantasized he was a cowboy who rode off into the sunset. Ironically, Steve later discovered his father was a hard-living biker—not far off from a modern-day cowboy.

If not supplied satisfying information, our minds fill in with stories. You might have needed to create certain fantasies to survive childhood pain, but you're strong enough to handle the truth now. It might even set you free. If your family was like mine, and Mom was keeper of the facts, you might take a giant stride in your relationship with her by admitting she was right all along.

# Friends as Family

**M**ost of us have different sets of friends as we journey through life. We may not realize it, but we end up choosing friends who either give us things we lacked at home or remind us in some way of what was there.

One of the first friends I can remember was Ronnie Rasche. Ronnie lived outside the projects where we lived when I was in grade school. "Inside vs. outside the projects" was a big deal in my childhood. The school officials would line us up to walk home and if you were a projects kid, everyone would assume your family couldn't keep a job.

We all grow up not knowing if what goes on in our family is "normal" until we see other families in action. And Ronnie's family was one of the first I experienced that didn't have Anderson as a last name. (Invariably, I went to *his* house—Ronnie didn't come to mine because of my dad's drinking. You never knew what your friends would find and it was just too risky.)

Ronnie lived in a pretty poor section even though it wasn't the projects. I remember going over there and the instant comparisons that went on in my mind. He had older brothers and sisters like mine, but they were nice to me. *Of course* they were nice to me—they weren't my brothers and sisters. They tormented Ronnie, though—after all, he was their brother. I remember thinking that my family's house—well, duplex—was newer and being relieved that at least we had *something* going for us. But still, I liked going over there. It was almost like trying on a new family for a while. Of course, I developed new friends as I grew up and eventually lost touch with Ronnie. But his sister came to my show in Vegas a few years ago, and I was genuinely happy to see her and glad to hear news of him.

Some of the friends I collected after Ronnie were part of the wild period I went through in high school. Hey, you have to have partners in crime! But after I got arrested for stealing hot snowmobiles, my probation officer referred me to a job where I counseled kids at a treatment center. I worked the night shift and that's where I met someone who'd become a longtime friend and help me on a path that would change my life.

Jim Gitar, one of the shift supervisors, was calm, stable, and encouraging. Becoming friends with him was tantamount to getting a free therapist. He was the first older male I'd met who had the appearance of stability, and as such he became a kind of father figure. Later, as I entered the crazy world of stand-up comedy, he was frequently there as my touchstone. It was sort of like that scene in *Rocky* where Rocky explains why he and Adrian would make a good team. We "filled gaps."

That's what Jim and some of my other friends have done. They've replaced what was missing in my family.

I've had other special friendships in my adulthood that seemed fated to help me get where I needed to go. I've had many agents and managers—perhaps *too* many (these relationships can often mimic too closely that of a family). My agent Tracy Kramer, who represented me for many years, also helped me on a spiritual path. Yes, a spiritual agent.

Tracy advised me to choose what was good for my soul, rather than what might be profitable in the short term. At one point, for example, I was offered a lot of money to write an autobiography, but the book I *wanted* to write was a series of letters to my deceased father. Tracy told me to do what was in my heart, and that series of letters, titled *Dear Dad,* went on to get great reviews and become a best-seller—something I'm still proud of.

Tracy also urged me to create an animated series, which other agents might have scoffed at. Even after we'd both gone our separate ways professionally, he pushed to get *Life with Louie* done, knowing it was important for his family issues, my family issues, and what has turned out to be family issues for many others.

Years ago, I met a fan at the Comedy Store whom, in retrospect, I seemed destined to meet. Jhoni Marchinko and I established an instant connection as two survivors of rough childhoods where the soup had definitely been overcooked. She saw my humor as a cleaned-up, palatable version of what she knew to be a very difficult situation. What attracted me to Jhoni was her wry wit. It was the dark, cynical side of my humor coin. After my gigs, we'd drive around the city talking for hours—and we supported each other by being consistent, honest, and most of all, making each other laugh.

Jhoni became my friend, my assistant, and then my friend again. Not always an easy transition to make. After working for me, Jhoni became comedian Marty Engel's assistant. And then one day she revealed her hidden passion—she told me she wanted to do stand-up herself. I encouraged her, but it's almost impossible for a would-be stand-up comedian to gain any traction in a city where you can see Jay Leno, Eddie Murphy, or Jerry Seinfeld on any given night.

I told Jhoni that if she wanted to make her dream happen, she should go back to Minnesota where she could get stage time. I loaned her twenty thousand dollars to support herself while she got her chops down. She lived in modest quarters, played my old haunts, and a year and a half later returned to L.A. and became a regular at the Improv. Jhoni was (and is) funny. But in stand-up, being funny is not the only ingredient of success and recognition. You have to develop an embrace-able point of view. This, unfortunately, only happens on the Great Stand-up God in the Sky's timetable. There's nothing you can do, nothing you can learn, no magic wand to speed the process. In my opinion, Jhoni's main shortcoming was her lack of needing the audience to accept her. In that respect, I guess she's too healthy.

So after giving it a good try, even garnering appearances on national television shows, another hidden passion arose. Writing. And this seemed to click immediately. When I got a television show for CBS that was being executive produced by *Murphy Brown*'s creator Diane English, I immediately asked Diane to hire Jhoni as a writer. That series was eventually canceled, but Jhoni went on to write for such shows as *Murphy Brown, Ellen,* and ultimately *Will & Grace,* where her sparkling lines won her a position as coexecutive producer. Jhoni recently signed a seven-figure deal with a studio, but she'd long since paid me back the twenty thousand dollars that I'd loaned her.

There are many stories in Hollywood of mentor-protégé relationships where the positions equaled out, or the student even surpassed the teacher, leaving the two

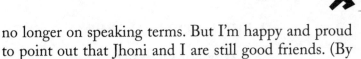

no longer on speaking terms. But I'm happy and proud to point out that Jhoni and I are still good friends. (By the way, she should know I'm still in charge.)

More recently, I've let someone into my life who's had a tremendous impact on me. Despite my having lived in L.A. for twenty years, most of my close friends hail from the place I grew up, Minnesota. Maybe it's that we have common roots and values, but I just find it easier to trust a Vikings fan. (It's sometimes easier than trusting the Vikings themselves, who've broken all our hearts too many times.) My friend's name is Abraham Geisness, and his special skill is calling me on my screwups. In holding me accountable to him, he holds me accountable to myself, my stand-up, my rhetoric, to the things I believe in—especially my aspiration to have a better family life.

There's one thing comedians abhor more than anything and that's hypocrisy. Abraham walks his own talk of trying to live a moral life, and he holds me accountable to the philosophy I spew.

How do all these friends relate back to family? The friends we choose along the way become our temporary family. Sometimes in rough periods they provide emotional shelter. Sometimes, of course, we clone the same dysfunctional family situation we were born into. Just as we try on suits to see how we look in them, friends are often temporary, becoming permanent only when we're sure the fit is right.

Frequently, we treat our friends better than our families. But we should cut our families some slack. Our friends don't have all that history nor do they know all our secrets.

## FAMILY SURVIVAL TIPS

### (for my friends)

**#34 Mirror, mirror.** Choosing friends is a way of mirroring yourself, not only on the outside but on the inside. Your true friends will be honest with you in a way your family may not. Asking your parents for an assessment of your strengths and weaknesses is likely to deliver the same accuracy as if you said, "Mirror, mirror, on the wall, who's the greatest kid of all?" Mom and Dad have an investment in seeing you a certain way so that they, in turn, can see themselves as certain types of parents. But friends, the down-and-dirty Denny's buddies you can *really* talk to—they'll tell you when you're getting fat, when you're taking too much crap from your boss, when you're being a jerk with that girl you like.

**#35 Friendship check.** Look at the friends you've chosen over the years. How have they reflected your family? In what ways are they similar? Did they add something to your life that your own family lacked? Sometimes we work backward and use things we've learned in friendships to create healthier relationships with our family. A friend who grew up in a more functional family can sometimes have valuable lessons to pass on.

# Family In-Laws

*"After three days, food and in-laws both start to stink."*

**W**hy is it often so hard to get along with mother- and father-in-laws, the people who gave birth to the person we fell in love with? Well, look at it from *their* perspective: You stole their child. You won the prize.

The parents hold the trophy—their son or daughter— for so many years, but eventually it has to be put on someone else's mantel. Trouble inevitably results because the parents want to remind you *they* were the ones who owned that trophy for twenty-five years and this is how things *used* to be. It's only because of *them* that you got such a good kid in the first place so don't be mad at them for wanting him or her back for a few days (which can turn into a few weeks or what seems like a lifetime).

Since most parents profess to wanting nothing but happiness for their child, it's ironic that they sometimes spend years making their child miserable by being the difficult in-law. Sometimes, though, this tricky situation is a setup perpetrated in part by a spouse.

Take, for example, the husband whose mother applauded every time he finished his peas or made doo-doo on the potty. He's not going to give up that ceaseless stream of approbation so easily. So, though he's paying for his mom's airfare, he just happens to let her

book her own reservation, fully knowing she'll "accidentally" get the dates wrong and that those four days she's supposed to stay during the Christmas holiday will stretch to two weeks because, "well, it was a lower fare and I felt so guilty having you pay for that expensive ticket." Face it, secretly the husband *likes* his wife and his mother fighting over him. And he may also like his wife's protecting him from the one woman in the world he has no power over—his mother.

Or take the wife who's always been "Daddy's little girl." I'm sure she doesn't mind the bidding war for her affections that goes on during the holidays. So what if her husband bought her that diamond tennis bracelet. Her *father* got her that sweater with the aardvark on it, which made her cry since it evoked a fond memory of going to the zoo with him twenty years ago.

Sometimes when we first meet in-laws, we get along surprisingly well. In fact, we may believe we're finally getting a chance to experience a fantasy family by marrying into it. Our new relatives seem to handle things so differently from our own family. Then inevitably something happens and disillusionment sets in. *Why can't they handle things like* my *family?*

When we initially meet our in-laws, we may be drawn by the "any family but mine" appeal. At such times, it's important to listen to warnings issued by our prospective spouses. Why? Because our in-laws are too smart to scare off any suitors. They'll be on their best behavior because they don't want to scare away a potential money-earner, scapegoat, and child-bearer/sperm donor.

We should prick up our ears when our fiancée speaks, because we'll learn a lot:

"Listen, my aunt Mary will come on to you with her

big breasts even though she's seventy-six. My brother Dave will want to arm wrestle you two-out-of-three for the championship. And my dad will try to persuade you that hunting with assault rifles is a good thing."

We should listen to these things, but chances are we'll fall under the hypnotic spell of this not being *our* family. We'll think Aunt Mary is a sweet, charming, harmless flirt. That we could beat Dave if we had another shot at the title. And that until talking with our spouse's father, we never realized how overpopulated the country is with deer.

Cut to a year later when we're giving our own family members the same warning we once received . . . and meanwhile, looking for ways to avoid having Aunt Mary French kiss us, wincing at the prospect of Dave extending his meaty forearm, and desperately trying to duck a meeting of our father-in-law's pro-Bambi-killing fringe faction of the NRA.

I do realize there are those who have *wonderful* mother- and father-in-laws who may even be better to pal around with than the parents one grew up with. As is the case with good families, this probably occurs more than people think, but you don't hear much about it because everyone is so busy enjoying himself. And maybe it's a good thing people in these blissful situations keep quiet. What would stand-up comedians do without all those mother-in-law jokes?

Of course, parents-in-law are only one side of the equation. What about families out there who are welcoming new sons- and daughters- and brothers- and sisters-in-law? It seems to me that these fall into three types: the Welcome-to-the-Family-in-Law, the Not-What-We-Expected-But-Tolerated-in-Law, and the Outlaw-in-Law.

The Welcome-to-the Family-in-Law is immediately embraced. This is the son-in-law Greg who knows how to install those storm windows your dad always wanted you to put in, and goes fishing with your old man and actually seems to be interested in his story about the giant muskee that got away. Or the beautiful daughter-in-law Judy whom Mom immediately takes shopping and is suddenly the only one Mom listens to about whether that new Ann Taylor ensemble really makes her look younger.

Sometimes these types of in-laws can produce jealousy in existing siblings. *How come we never got this treatment?* Keep in mind these new family members don't come with the baggage everyone else in the family is carrying. They never got caught smoking in the basement after they set fire to Mom's favorite pillow or ruined the whole family's vacation plans by flunking bio and having to take summer school. But the envy these accepted in-laws bring can be productive in getting everyone to realize the things that were previously missing in the family. Maybe it's time to learn how to install those storm windows so you can help Dad out too.

The Tolerated-in-Law is a stable choice whom the family might not have picked, but who doesn't keep everyone up at night worrying. He or she is included in family functions and usually slips under the radar of familial scrutiny. Sure, you may miss hearing how incredible your spouse is every time you walk in the door. On the other hand, you can breathe easy knowing no one in the family is gunning for him or her. Relax and enjoy the lack of drama. This type of in-law sometimes occurs in families who weren't really looking to add extra members. Unlike the previous type, they're not filling a void that was missing in the family.

There are two types of Outlaw-in-Laws. One you may recognize from an episode of *America's Most Wanted,* and, well, that's a tricky one. I don't really know what to tell you there—except call that 800 number and turn him in. But the other Outlaw-in-Law is a rugged individualist who has her own opinion of who they are. They want acceptance on *their* terms and are not looking to immediately conform to family expectations. I've heard more than one story where these types of Outlaw-in-Laws later became important members of the family, frequently after initial heated arguments.

Both this second type of Outlaw-in-Law and the host family can learn valuable lessons from each other. In one family I know, two daughters married two very different types of husbands. The doctor son-in-law whom everyone initially greeted with open arms turned out to be too consumed with his work to become part of their lives. Meanwhile, the motorcycle-riding rebel who'd gone from job to job wound up coming into the family business and helping to save it when his father-in-law passed away.

My main point about each of these in-laws is to stay open. You never know whom you're actually getting. And sometimes that Outlaw-in-Law becomes the most welcome member of the family.

## SURVIVAL FAMILY TIP

### (for mother-in-laws who are not a joke)

**#36 Meet the parents.** Here's my quick advice about conflicts with parents-in-law: You can't win, you can only limit the time you endure the process. When visiting or having them visit, enjoy this time when you're not the center of attention. Eventually your spouse will remember *why* he or she left their family. If you're constantly getting into fights with your spouse over your in-laws, take the emphasis off being mad for a moment and ask yourself if your spouse is setting this up for his or her own reasons.

Those of you who fall instantly in love with your in-laws, remember the exciting family that is so much more spontaneous than yours today may reveal themselves to be irresponsible spend-thrifts who're driving you crazy tomorrow. Don't blame your spouse for not warning you.

On the other hand, that in-law you can't stand could turn out to be the one who surprises you most. Someone once told me this story of how their uncle Mark married this woman June whom no one could stand. A few weeks after the ceremony, Mark had a heart attack and died. June ended up doing a wonderful job raising Mark's daughter Donna from a previous marriage and was eventually accepted as a true member of Mark's extended family.

# Family Finances

Acouple years ago Oprah Winfrey was in the planning stages of a show that would focus on how family members deal with the financial aspects of having someone successful in the family. Oprah's producers spotted my sister Sally and my brother Kyle on *48 Hours* talking about their relationship with me, and called to invite all of us to appear on *Oprah*. We were preinterviewed, but encouraged not to speak with each other before taping our segment. I'd been granting my relatives' requests for money for years, but until that afternoon, hadn't discussed with any of them my feelings about it.

Money is an issue for every family—one that too often doesn't get talked about. Proverbial wisdom holds that poor people know better how to stretch and save a dollar because they must do more with less. This definitely wasn't the case in the Anderson household. If we got some money, it was gone. We were always robbing Peter to pay Paul. Or the money might be spent on my dad's drinking or his bingo playing. (Who do you think I learned my gambling from?)

Just because I acquired a pretty good earning capacity as an adult doesn't mean I knew what to do with the money I made. What I *do* know is that as soon as I started to make some serious bucks, the calls for money started coming in. I've felt privileged to be in a position to help out my mother, siblings, nieces, and nephews financially. In truth, the money doesn't mean that much to me. And yet, the emotions behind the money sometimes drag me down. Often, there's a feeling of betrayal or dishonesty—sometimes, it's simply a feeling of being used.

So here in a nutshell is how *The Oprah Winfrey Show* went. There were three segments. One featured a twenty-seven-year-old kid who'd struck it rich working for AOL. Another focused on someone who'd won a million dollars on some TV game show. The last was the segment on the Andersons. Oprah brought us out and asked my siblings what they thought about me and my money. Kyle freely admitted he'd be quite happy if, financially, I just took care of him for the rest of his life. I wasn't mad at hearing that. I just thought he was being honest. Sally said she was grateful for the money I gave her, and I'm sure she meant that too. But I confessed that I felt somewhat used in this whole money exchange—that people continued to call me for cash and each time they acted like they were entitled.

Oprah herself could relate. She mentioned that she had relatives who expected her to buy them a house. They'd gone as far as picking their own Christmas presents. Clearly, this issue hit a nerve with her. With all the money she has, she must grapple with it more often than I. And unlike the other two "successes" on the show, she and I had been dealing with the situation for years. During the show, I also mentioned that I'd gotten to the point where I felt my relatives *only* cared about me for the money. It was that comment that got me in the most trouble. Maybe it's not true, but sometimes it sure feels that way.

Though they enjoyed being on *Oprah*, Sally and Kyle both felt uneasy after seeing the finished show. Sally thought the show had been edited in such a way that she didn't get to express how much she loved me—money or no money. She told me I should be able to say "no" when people call and ask. The problem is this: Each time I say "no" I feel a sense of guilt. *Am I not a good brother/uncle?* If I have my assistant field the call, then I'm impersonal. If I do it myself, I can be wiped out emotionally for days. It's also disappointing to see that the money doesn't go toward something that would improve the long-term outlook. It's usually requested when things are at their worst: a health emergency, an inability to make rent, a car problem. I'd feel better if the money were going toward college or some sort of training to get them out of their situation.

Being the one who hands out the money also puts me in the role of father figure, which I don't relish. It's like being the father with none of the rewards.

I don't blame my brothers and sisters. This is what we saw growing up: Get money, spend money. Get money, spend money. When you're living on government cheese (which is delicious, by the way), you're not investing in mutual funds. That's one of the main problems with housing projects. There's no surer way to keep people poor than to surround them with other poor people.

As I've mentioned previously in this book, I find it interesting that my sister Sally, who grew up with our rich uncle, still displays many of her siblings' traits, including trouble keeping a dollar. Some of her fondest memories of my father are when he'd buy her a new dress or some shoes. Money is relative. My uncle's buying her things didn't mean as much as my dad's doing so. The latter meant more to her because my dad's money was rare and hard-won.

As a family, we grew up with such scarcity that I sometimes wonder if being poor is what we're most comfortable with. Unconsciously, that was the message my dad sent whenever he squandered an opportunity to get us out of our dire financial situation.

Since *The Oprah Winfrey Show*, I've given more thought to what's really underneath the money I give to my relatives. Do I give it because I feel guilty that I got the breaks and they didn't? Do I do it to pay homage to my mother by taking care of her children? Or do I give cash because it's easier than giving myself?

As for why my siblings feel so entitled to the money, I'll let you in on a little secret. Mine was *not* a typical blue-collar family. In my mother's mind—and thus in ours—my father was royalty. He'd been famous. And that meant one day we'd regain our rightful place among the well-to-do. Perhaps that's why we Andersons always believe we're about to hit the jackpot. It's our destiny.

Which brings me to my final confession about money. As you've heard before, I like to gamble. A lot. I could easily chalk this up to some addictive genetic predisposition. But I wonder if my gambling is a way of accomplishing a three-fold purpose: a) getting rid of money I feel guilty for having in the first place, b) making sure no one else gets the money or asks for it, which would require me to either say "no" and feel guilty or "yes" and feel used, and c) keeping me close to my father whom I used to play Bingo with.

I'll lay you five-to-one odds I've guessed right.

• • •

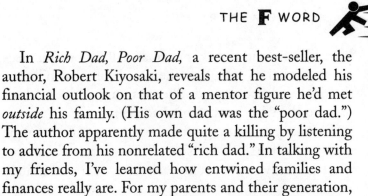

In *Rich Dad, Poor Dad,* a recent best-seller, the author, Robert Kiyosaki, reveals that he modeled his financial outlook on that of a mentor figure he'd met *outside* his family. (His own dad was the "poor dad.") The author apparently made quite a killing by listening to advice from his nonrelated "rich dad." In talking with my friends, I've learned how entwined families and finances really are. For my parents and their generation, it was considered taboo to discuss money at all. No one ever discussed salaries. This was before Forbes listed the four hundred richest Americans, before Gordon Gekko proclaimed "greed is good," before people knew the financial stats of sports heroes as well as their batting averages. I once had an accountant whose father told him that "money is just people's way of saying thank you." Well, that's a nice thought—but not very practical when you're swimming with the sharks in the business world.

My friend Sharon had a father who was very generous and not at all tight-fisted about money. However, he'd always borrow whatever the family needed. Instead of buying his own tools, he'd show up at the neighbors and ask if they happened to have a power drill or a lathe they weren't using. When they'd go on vacation, instead of getting a hotel room, her father would call up long-lost relatives he hadn't spoken to in years and let them know he'd be in the area and could use a room for him and the family. This was particularly embarrassing since there were three kids. He was a school teacher who received his last paycheck at the summer's beginning, and as the summer went along Sharon would notice how meals would increasingly consist of long forgotten items dredged from the back of food cupboards.

Many years later, Sharon's father developed a serious

liver ailment, and to help out financially, it became necessary for her to look into the details of what bills her dad had and hadn't paid. She was amazed to see how close to the edge her parents had been living.

For many families, getting by is almost like a magic act. It might help if we shared the secrets of finances more honestly so we could learn from each generation's mistakes.

The other day a strange—but weirdly appealing—thought occurred to me. What if money were lettuce? Imagine carrying around heads of lettuce, peeling off leaves to pay for your everyday needs. We'd be forced to use Ziploc wallets to keep the lettuce from spoiling. But since it *is* highly perishable, we'd have to spend it quickly rather than hoard it. And, perhaps given that, if we saw people who had *no* lettuce, we'd be more inclined to give them some of ours.

This notion may sound silly—okay, it *is* silly—but money is only what we perceive it to be, and believe me, the arguments people have with their families about money can seem equally silly.

## FAMILY SURVIVAL TIPS

### (for the big money)

**#37 The real treasure hunt.** It's important to look at the emotions that lie behind your attitude toward money. Are you remaining the impoverished offspring because you're still mad at your dad for not taking care of you when you were a kid? I know a young woman who last year had a nervous breakdown at age thirty-three. In the

past, her father had been this cheap, withholding guy who wouldn't even pay for the braces she needed. My friend's breakdown forced her father to make a choice: either let his daughter be out on the street or step in and financially support her. The father ended up paying his daughter's rent for a year. What this woman really wanted most was to have her dad take care of her. She's put her life back together, but her emotional balance will be short-lived if she doesn't realize her dad will never be able to go back to her childhood and fix those wounds.

**#38 Change the message on your answering machine.** This is where I'm supposed to tell you it's okay to say "no" if you're the responsible family member who's continually being asked for money. But I understand how hard that is. I advise you to look more closely at what your relatives are after. Your time? Your attention? Those who're borrowing should do the same. If you can deduce what's really going on, you can better respond to the situation and know whether the money will help. Also, estimate how much irresponsibility you can take from the person you're lending to and plan accordingly. Vow to give them "X" dollars this time, "Y" dollars the next time, and then cut them off. But don't beat yourself up if emotions triumph over intellect and you deviate from the plan. After all, they're family and this is hard stuff.

To those in the position of borrowing money, I offer the story of the millionaire who lent a hundred dollars to several ghetto kids. The kid who worked hard to pay him back promptly is the one he trusted. And so, the urban myth goes, the millionaire ended up sending that young man to college.

If you find yourself in a situation where you're borrowing all the time, ask yourself what you can do to change the patterns that have put you in this spot. Realize it's often uncomfortable for *both* parties to be in this situation. The best way to say "thank you" is to honor your agreements and make every effort to avoid being financially dependent in the future.

To those doing the lending, my advice would be to appreciate the vulnerabilities of your relatives and try not to flaunt your good fortune or tie your good acts to conditions. If you're going to do a good deed, do it for its own reward. I've always found that money given this way comes back tenfold.

# Family Luck

Allen was always wearing lucky underwear. He found that when he'd wear certain well-worn pairs, he'd have a better day. So the holes in those pairs got bigger and bigger, and his wife, seeing what he was putting on in the morning, got more and more embarrassed.

Where does this superstitious behavior come from? Well, say you're a kid and you're playing tennis with your dad who's always beaten you. But on this day, your serve is hot and you're acing him left and right. How to explain it? I mean, he's your *dad*—the one who taught you how to play. How can this be happening?

Your father, who still wants to be the man in charge, simply says, "Hey, kid, you got lucky." You don't mind this explanation because as long as you got lucky, you can *stay* a kid and don't have to admit you've surpassed your dad. Because if you've surpassed your dad, then who'll be there to take care of you?

Sometimes it's easier to attribute our success or failure to external reasons. Many people will glibly say, "I control my own destiny." But that implies responsibility. If you buy into the premise that success or failure begins with you, you have to credit or blame that person in the mirror for what occurs. It's a philosophy that compels the person holding it to be a grown-up. In other words, it's a world view people like Allen, with his lucky underwear fixation, may not yet be willing to embrace.

I've always considered myself lucky in many ways, especially when it comes to my career. But I also know how much work has gone into my success. A colleague who wrote a hit movie told me that when the movie succeeded, some of his siblings treated him like he'd just gotten lucky, implying his achievement had little to do with him. They seemed to think it was just a matter of his eating a different breakfast cereal that day. They discounted the years he lived in a one-room apartment struggling, his forgoing law school and being willing to take a huge chance with his future, the hours and hours he'd spent writing screenplays that hadn't sold.

The danger of equating success with luck is that it doesn't acknowledge the work we must do to achieve our goals. Similarly, people can feel they're "cursed," and thus not put in the effort that could extricate them from their situation.

### FAMILY SURVIVAL TIP
#### (for those who like to roll the dice)

**#39 The lucky underwear is you.** As Clint Eastwood says in *Dirty Harry*, "Ask yourself, punk, do you feel lucky?" If you're attributing too much of your success to external factors, examine whether you were unconsciously undermined by your parents growing up. It probably wasn't on purpose. They were just insecure themselves. Feel free now to give yourself credit for what you've earned.

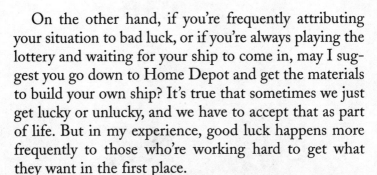

On the other hand, if you're frequently attributing your situation to bad luck, or if you're always playing the lottery and waiting for your ship to come in, may I suggest you go down to Home Depot and get the materials to build your own ship? It's true that sometimes we just get lucky or unlucky, and we have to accept that as part of life. But in my experience, good luck happens more frequently to those who're working hard to get what they want in the first place.

I just had an uncomfortable thought, by the way. My gambling—is that a way of denying my actual accomplishments and trusting my fate to luck?

# Fame

Jim Carrey, Argus Hamilton, Blake Clark, Paul Rodriguez, Andrew Dice Clay, me, and Harry Basil hanging at The Comedy Store. (Courtesy The Comedy Store)

People sometimes ask me where I got started. I'm going to tell you, but I also want to tell you *why* I got started and why I kept going. How we map our career reveals a lot about our family. Our workplace relationships, whether formed hanging at the Comedy Store or at the office watercooler, also reveal a lot. For as I've pointed out, we take our families with us everywhere.

I got into comedy on a dare. I was working at the treatment center when someone dared me to get up onstage at a small club in Minneapolis called Mickey Finn's. I remember it as all coming pretty naturally to

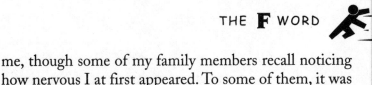

me, though some of my family members recall noticing how nervous I at first appeared. To some of them, it was surprising I was the one doing comedy since my brother Kyle had always been "the funny one" in the family.

Onstage, I knew I had to deal with my size right off the bat. So I'd start with lines like "I can't stay long. I'm between meals." It let the audience know I was aware of how big I was; I got them on my side so we could all go down this path together. I always kept my act clean because I was playing to people in Minneapolis and knew they wouldn't approve if I swore. In the end, what hardened my resolve to "make it" was that those first audiences liked me. I'd gotten a taste of approval and wanted more.

Many of those who go into show business are looking for the attention they never got at home, and I was no different. Of course, I didn't get immediate acceptance from my family. It wasn't until people came up to my parents and siblings and started saying things like "how proud you must be of Louie" that it dawned on them, "I guess he *is* good." Their eventual acceptance of me as a performer made me feel both relieved (that they finally respected what I was trying to do) and at the same time disappointed (that it was my *achievements* they were praising and not necessarily *me*).

In her book *The Drama of the Gifted Child,* Alice Miller discusses the problems faced by successful adults who experience an underlying emptiness because they feel it's their accomplishments, rather than their actual selves, that their parents loved. Many of those adults displayed special talents or skills at an early age. As children, they wanted to ask their parents, "Would you still love me if I were dirty or angry or anything but this perfect child?" Unfortunately, they were too scared of losing their parents' love to actually pop the question. So they worked even harder to create the persona of "wonderful person."

Maybe that's what I created onstage so everyone, including my parents, would love me.

**An early headshot**

**Louie Anderson**

Every job requires a certain amount of rejection and humiliation. But the amount of rejection and humiliation one must go through in show business is so great it tends to attract those who've already "been there" in their own childhood. Ironically—or perhaps not so ironically—coming from a dysfunctional family makes it easier to withstand the pain of being turned down at hundreds of auditions, of standing before a crowd that's not laughing at your jokes, of listening to total strangers trash your latest movie or TV show. What person from a *normal* family would go through all this?

It was by no means a sure thing that I wound up where I eventually did. Growing up, I never dreamed of being a comedian. But one of the few things my dad and I shared was watching Johnny Carson. Being a trumpeter, Dad always appreciated Doc Severinsen. At least, his playing if not his fashion choices. So when I started doing comedy, my big goal was to be on Johnny Carson's *Tonight Show.*

To do that, I knew I'd have to move to Los Angeles.

## First Time in L.A.

My first mistake on the road to fame and fortune was to think Hollywood was the same as St. Paul. Upon arriving in L.A., I moved in with another comic and his wife. I really liked this comic, but he could be mean and competitive. Meanwhile, his wife was a very nice Minnesotan. Maybe "the town" had just gotten to this guy. You hear those two words a lot in L.A. "You have to drive a nice car in *this town.*" "*This town* will make you crazy." "I got to get out of *this town.*" But I was still caught up in the excitement of it all.

My immediate goal was to get a gig at the world

famous Comedy Store on Sunset where Richard Pryor, Robin Williams, Eddie Murphy, and hundreds of other famous comedians have played. I'd go there on open-mike nights where amateurs get to wait for hours to do three minutes of material for free. But the club's owner, Mitzi Shore (whom some may also know as Pauley Shore's mother), paid me no attention whatsoever.

Then one night Jimmie Walker, the "dy-no-mite" star of *Good Times,* saw me and made Mitzi watch. Jimmie has been responsible for helping lots of people, including giving David Letterman and me writing jobs early on. The next week, Mitzi made me a regular and I started performing three or four times a week in the Original Room, which held at maximum about one hundred and fifty people. The show started at 8:00 P.M. and I usually went on about 8:15 right after Harris Peet, the emcee-doorman. Most of the time there were only four people in the audience, but who cared. I was at the Comedy Store in Hollywood. Maybe someone would discover me.

I had this time slot for a while but eventually grew exasperated, since I realized it wasn't until 9:00 at the earliest that all the agents and managers arrived—not to mention the guy who booked *The Tonight Show.* Then I made friends with a woman named Debbie who called all the comics to tell them their time slots. Luckily, she was from Minnesota and had Mitzi's ear. Debbie confided that I'd only get the better slot if an agent, casting person, or a manager let Mitzi know they wanted to check me out. I couldn't get anyone to see me so I decided to make up a person.

I was just about to have some fake person call when I heard that someone from *The Tonight Show* was coming down to see Howie Mandel. I begged Debbie to put

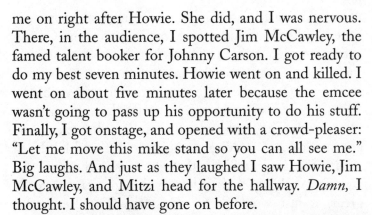

me on right after Howie. She did, and I was nervous. There, in the audience, I spotted Jim McCawley, the famed talent booker for Johnny Carson. I got ready to do my best seven minutes. Howie went on and killed. I went on about five minutes later because the emcee wasn't going to pass up his opportunity to do his stuff. Finally, I got onstage, and opened with a crowd-pleaser: "Let me move this mike stand so you can all see me." Big laughs. And just as they laughed I saw Howie, Jim McCawley, and Mitzi head for the hallway. *Damn*, I thought. I should have gone on before.

After Howie got on Carson, I thought maybe he'd put in a good word for me. And he did, but Jim McCawley wasn't easily swayed, and any time I saw him he always seemed to look right through me. I was persistent, though, and I finally got him to come back and watch my act. Actually, he came after my agent (whom I'd subsequently gotten), Mitzi herself, and some of my fellow comics told him how great I was. After I auditioned for Jim at the club, I went over and thanked him for coming. The rule is, a comic *never* asks someone how he's done onstage. You let your agent or manager handle it.

I called my agent the next day to hear what I hoped was good news. I found out I wasn't *Tonight Show* material. I was devastated. I figured my career was over and one of my goals would never be achieved. I kept getting McCawley to come and see my act, but he always said he didn't think Johnny would like me.

For two years this went on, and then one night the talent booker for *Late Night with David Letterman* was at the Store. I didn't even know it. She came up to me after my set and said they'd love to have me on the show. I told her my agent's name and the next day they called with a confirmed date. Guess what? Jim McCawley also called and offered me a confirmed date on the Carson show. And it was a date *before* the Letterman show. I thought this was great, having no idea the two shows competed. (Back then, the turf wars were less visible.)

As it turned out, the people at the Letterman show were livid. They told me that if I did Carson, my appearance on *Late Night* would be canceled. I felt I had to do *The Tonight Show*, though. It was the show I'd watched with my dad and even though Dave is really great, it just wouldn't be the same. The Letterman people said they'd understand, but they were mad and I couldn't get on for the next two years. I don't know if I did the right thing, but my mom was still alive and she wouldn't know Letterman. This would be the biggest moment of my life.

(Courtesy Carson Entertainment)

I went on my first *Tonight Show* November 20, 1984. After my set, I went back to the dressing room and some stagehand started chasing me. Johnny wanted me to come back out for a second bow. He didn't ask me to sit down, but I went over and shook his hand. After the show, Johnny popped into my dressing room, breaking from his entourage, and told me, "You did great, kid." To this day, that means a lot to me. I was told that Johnny loved me, and I guess he must have because I did six more *Tonight Show*s in the next nine months. Jim McCawley was nice to me, but we didn't really settle things till much later. I still couldn't get on *Letterman* so I wrote Dave a letter. In it, I suggested that if he were in the same situation, he'd do the same thing. Not long after that, I got on the show and Dave has always been very nice to me.

I sometimes wonder if I would have put myself on another career path if I'd done the hipper Letterman show first. Would it have made me a different, perhaps happier comic? A career in Hollywood is full of choices and politics that can make Washington's smoke-filled back rooms seem like preschool. Especially before cable when Carson was king, a comic could easily ruin his career in one day. In the end, I consider myself lucky.

### Family and Career

In show business you tend to find many surrogate family members, and after a while I became part of Mitzi's extended family of comics. She started to warm to me after I did a pilot for Mike Douglas, the talk show host. (This was before my *Tonight Show* break.) I didn't have a nice sports coat so for my first performances I showed up in a gray sweater. When someone asked me if that was what I was wearing, I said it was my image and that Billy Cosby always wore sweaters. (Is it just a coincidence that both he and I do warm material about families?) After that, if I played the Comedy Store and wore a sports jacket, Mitzi would come up and say that I was a sweater guy.

Sometimes I'd have to follow acts like Robin Williams, Eddie Murphy, or Sam Kinnison who really worked the audience into a frenzy. I had to figure out how to deal with them. Usually, I'd face the crowd and keep saying "one more time for Robin Williams." I'd do this until they were thinking *Hey, that's enough already.*

I mean, you can only praise someone so much. Even if it were Elvis, people would eventually say, "that's enough." I learned that by watching Johnny Carson. When a star was too big to stay for the whole show, Johnny would thank them and talk about them until you'd start mumbling, "I love Bob Hope, but what's next."

I had little control over my ego so I'm sure that, after a star like Eddie Murphy had just left the stage, some part of me was trying to take my game to another level. (It's not too different from wanting to measure up to the sibling who's just hit a home run or scored an A on the test.) Every comic thinks he is the funniest. It bugs them that a fellow comic is more popular. If they don't admit it, they're liars. Comedy is all about ego, all about being the greatest. The comics I've found myself competing with are the ones who are truly funny. I'm not threatened by comics who don't have a point of view.

I realize *your* career is probably much different than mine. But there's really no difference between handling egos in an office setting and handling them in a comedy club—or, for that matter, handling them at a family bar-

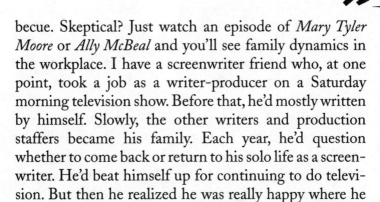

becue. Skeptical? Just watch an episode of *Mary Tyler Moore* or *Ally McBeal* and you'll see family dynamics in the workplace. I have a screenwriter friend who, at one point, took a job as a writer-producer on a Saturday morning television show. Before that, he'd mostly written by himself. Slowly, the other writers and production staffers became his family. Each year, he'd question whether to come back or return to his solo life as a screenwriter. He'd beat himself up for continuing to do television. But then he realized he was really happy where he was working because it had a great family atmosphere.

How many people do you know who love their work because they love the people they work with? How many people do you know who have problems with their boss that remarkably mirror their problems with their family?

I do corporate shows as a stand-up and I think sometimes big companies, whether they're accounting firms or tire manufacturers, don't realize how important a family atmosphere is to keeping their employees happy. Or maybe they do—and that's why they're "treating" their employees to a night of stand-up comedy and hiring me.

## FAMILY SURVIVAL TIPS

### (for those who want to be a star)

**#40 Find your point of view.** How does all of this about fame and career relate to family—aside from Mitzi's being a surrogate mom to me and many comics? The healthy thing about becoming a working comic is that it forces you to define *who* you are—at least, the public side of yourself. You *must* develop a point of view. I think that's healthy even for people who aren't stand-ups. You have to know *who* you are so you'll know what you want to say to people.

**#41 Acknowledge the bigger acts.** (At least the ones who *think* they are.) Yes, I had to deal with Robin Williams and Eddie Murphy. But doesn't your uncle Max think he's just as big a star? Or how about your sister-in-law Maggie—when she gets her hair done and has just come back from a Canyon Ranch health spa? Usually, it doesn't take much to placate their need for praise. Repeat after me: "Hey everyone, let's hear it for Maggie. Doesn't she look great? I mean it. *You* look fabulous." Okay, so you have to use just the right words or it'll sound insincere. But isn't a little forced enthusiasm better than listening to her drop subtle hints for two hours?

**#42 Treat yourself and your family members as stars.** When Dustin Hoffman once asked Laurence Olivier why he acted, Larry leaned over the table and whispered, "Look at me, look at me, look at me." We all like attention. I think certain people seek out fame and become stars so they can hold on to that feeling of being the kid who gets all the attention. (Or, as I mentioned earlier, so they can get the attention they never received in the first place.) Isn't that what flying first class is all about? You're paying people extra money just to be nicer to you. I always feel bad for the people back in coach. Sometimes, I'll even poke my head back through the curtain just to keep them updated. "We're eating now . . ."

Here's an idea. Every once in a while, what's wrong with treating yourself like a rock star? You've probably

heard about stars who write riders into their contracts requesting special items before a concert. Remember that band that required bowls of M&Ms in their dressing room with all the brown M&Ms taken out? Or the diva who needed to take a bath in milk before a show? Or the famous seventies band who asked for a "snowstorm"—their code word for cocaine—at every gig? I have a slightly more modest rider in my contracts that mandates I get a twelve-pack of Diet Coke, four two-liter bottles of Evian, two large bath-size towels, two hand-size towels, a deli platter, and a fruit platter before I go on.

You probably don't have roadies, but perhaps you have a significant other who can make sure you get your riders—so long as they get theirs in return. My advice is to learn from us crazy people in show business. Be specific in coming up with demands. I've even provided some examples to help get you started.

## Family Contract Riders

**Breakfast in bed.** I have to start my day right if you want me to be at my best . . .

[Here specify a lot of organic items that can only be found at a certain farmers' market, and only at 6:30 in the morning. Also, pick a coffee that's very hard to find. Most Hollywood folks find a small joint that's halfway across town, and get their assistants to run there and back without letting the joe get cold.]

**R&R.** Since I'm the one who holds this family together with all the work I do, I'm under incredible stress. I'll require a massage . . .

[Hollywood has massage specialists who've trained for years. If you can't find one in your yellow pages, try getting a device called the Thumper. No, it's not dirty. You can find it in catalogs and it has a long handle so your wife can massage her own back when you fall asleep.]

**Dealing with the press.** So that I feel everyone appreciates me, my accomplishments should be applauded and my opinion constantly sought . . .

[Real people actually have to pretend to *care* what others think. Stars know it's only what *they* say that counts. When talking to stars, careful attention should be paid to their egos (e.g., "Wow, honey, I really do love what you did with the living room—how *do* you do it?" . . . or "You've handled back-to-back carpools and met your deadline for that project at work—no wonder you're a superstar"). Of course, spend enough time playing the role of star, and you may find yourself saying, "I'm so sick of *me*. Let me hear about *you*." In Hollywood, that sort of transformation *has* happened— once or twice.]

**Groupies.** Regularly, I'll need to hand out backstage passes to my fans . . .

[Hopefully, the person you'll be handing the pass to is your spouse. Just let him or her know you picked them out of all the groupies waiting outside the tour bus. Let them know what you like and remind them that, next time, you'll be the one who's screaming to get near *them*.]

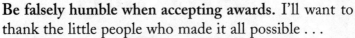

**Be falsely humble when accepting awards.** I'll want to thank the little people who made it all possible . . .

[Yes, of course, you'll want to thank your family, and heck, even your mother-in-law. But we all know who really deserves this award. You! Face it, without you, this picture couldn't have been made. Because you're the star of *this* family.]

# Free Billy the Kid

**M**y brother Billy suffered from schizophrenia. Some experts say this condition is caused or triggered by trauma so severe it causes your mind to close down and create a different personality or reality. It made me wonder what happened to Billy when he was a kid.

When I was a kid and my older brother acted weird or told some fantastic story, I mostly laughed because my friends were laughing. But there was a scary feeling going on somewhere behind my eyes, a sickness under my laugh down in the pit of my stomach. I knew something wasn't right about the way my brother was acting. Maybe my giggling friends knew too, but not like I knew, not like I felt. It would be easy to call it being embarrassed, but there was too much love there for my brother. It was closer to sadness, bordering on dread. Somewhere deep down, even though I was young, I sensed what was happening.

Because of the way families function, especially mine, I couldn't go to my parents and say "What's wrong with Billy, Mom and Dad? Why does he act the way he does?" The way a person handled things in my family was to stuff things down and cover them up. With me, it was covered up with food—lots and lots of food. Even

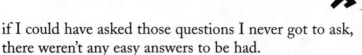

if I could have asked those questions I never got to ask, there weren't any easy answers to be had.

Billy was gone a lot. Often he was gone emotionally even when he was present. If I'd been one of the siblings who had to face my dad in the prime of his alcoholic rages, I would have been gone too. By the time I came along my dad had mellowed, though, believe me, he was still no Ward Cleaver.

It bothered the heck out of my mom when Billy would take off. He may have been the second oldest, but he was still her baby.

Even though Bill was a little crazy at times, he had that Anderson sense of humor. I often wonder how much being a little crazy is connected to humor. Think of how many times you've heard an audience member say of a comic onstage, "He's crazy." Martin Lawrence even titled his HBO special *You So Crazy*.

You always hear about the thin line between insanity and genius. Charlie Chaplin's mother was in a mental institution. Maybe part of comedy is helping people see that many of the things in this world that we accept as normal are, in fact, crazy. *Seinfeld* was popular because it showed people getting crazily caught up in life's minutiae. Letterman pokes fun at the absurdity of a talk show. Leno points out the stupidity of everyday things. And I've spent my adult life making jokes about my crazy family, which people continually tell me is just like theirs.

Anyway, back to Billy. There are some great stories about him. One time Frank and one of his friends hatched a plan to steal a backhoe, that piece of heavy equipment one often sees on a construction site, though this machine was on a farm. They needed a lookout so they took Billy along. Frank's plan was to load the backhoe onto a trailer after his friend had hot-wired it.

So they set out for the farm field where this perfect crime was to take place. They stationed Billy out by the road while Frank and Hot-Wire Willy went to work jump-starting the backhoe. Willy was still trying to work his magic when suddenly they heard noises you're *not* supposed to hear at three in the morning in the middle of a farm field. Frank pulled out his gun (the first time I heard this story, I was shocked to hear I had a brother who carried a gun), and the closer the sound got, the more tempted he was to shoot. By now, he'd identified the sound as coming from someone running through the field toward him.

Suddenly, whoever it was froze dead in his tracks. Frank kept his hand on the trigger, but realized no one was saying, "Halt, it's the police." Finally, he rose from his crouched shooting position. There, standing in the moonlight was Billy, wide-eyed with panic.

"What is it, Billy, did you see someone?" Frank asked.

"No," Billy answered.

"Then what the hell are you doing here?"

"I saw a spaceship. This is where the aliens pick you up."

Frank got really mad because they had no lookout and he'd almost shot his brother. The Anderson boys strike again. I won't mention whether or not they managed to lift the backhoe—since charges could still be pending.

It's strange, when I was a kid and my brother Billy would say he'd been picked up by an extraterrestrial, I'd immediately say, "Shut up! You *weren't* picked up by aliens!" But now that I'm older, I'm more liable to say, "Oh, really? Venus. What's the weather like up there?"

Billy's criminal career wasn't limited to backhoe pil-

fering. One time he decided to break open a safe at a department store. His plan was to go into the store while it was open, sneak into the storeroom, and hide in the area above the ceiling. So about an hour before closing he entered the store, secreted himself in the storeroom, and got settled in. After everyone had departed, he descended from his hiding spot and headed toward the safe. Everything was going according to plan, but when he got to the safe, he realized he'd forgotten his safecracking tools in his car. He went outside to retrieve them, forgetting that the door automatically locked when it closed. He wound up locking himself out of his own heist.

Billy—or Bill, as we called him later—spent a lot of his adult life searching for gold all along the West Coast. He liked to tell a story about the biggest gold nugget ever found, adding that he knew where there was an even bigger one. He wove an elaborate tale about a secret passage in the hills of Northern California. But whenever I asked him for specifics, he would cock his head, eye me suspiciously, and avoid answering. As if I, the laziest person in the world, might wait until he dozed off and then head out there to get it all for myself.

Even though everyone in the family heard a version of this story, we always tolerated it because, when Bill told it, his eyes were alive and he almost seemed completely well. And anyway, who knows? Maybe he *did* know where it was. Aren't we all in search of the world's biggest gold nugget?

Though his link to sanity always seemed tenuous, there was a sweetness to Bill. And an independence. He was the one member of my family whom I knew for sure hadn't been swayed by my fame. There was no jealousy there. He cared about me. Sometimes you find love in the most unlikely places.

I say "was" in referring to Billy because during the writing of this book, he died. I cried for a long time when that happened. I miss him very much.

He looked like a Kennedy, didn't he? I remember one time Bill gave me this great idea for a product I could endorse. Louie's Chewy Gooeys. Candy bars with double the sugar, double the fat: "Because life is hard."

Did the wife yell at you? Have a Louie's Chewy Gooey and forget about it. Mother-in-law coming to visit? Have a case. She's coming to *live* with you? Try our new Chewy Gooey by the truckload. Because life can be rough. So why not eat?

## FAMILY SURVIVAL TIP
## (for mental health)

**#43 Crazy is not *looking* at crazy.** I think the hardest aspect of mental illness is acknowledging it. Many families just ignore it, hoping it will go away. That only worsens the situation for those who are losing their bearings.

My friend Andrea's mother married a man named Reggie who suffered from bouts of paranoia and would claim government officials were breaking into his office and searching through his files. The family would go out to dinner and Reggie would insist that the waiters had put bugs in the ice cubes and were listening in on the conversation. Andrea's mother bent over backward to deny her new husband's increasing irrationality, fearing she'd lose her family. This in turn made Andrea think that perhaps her mother was the crazy one. Andrea deeply loved her mother and held no malice toward Reggie, but the rampant denial kept her from being closer to her mom. In the end, her mother wound up losing her family anyway.

The thing about coming from a background where mental illness is present is that even relatives who *don't* exhibit symptoms tend to wonder if they'll get it. I know a woman who had two brothers who were paranoid schizophrenics. Though she was a very successful, clear-thinking woman herself, she'd sometimes monitor her thoughts, checking her own sanity. Let's face it—we all get weirded out sometimes. Because so much of this is hereditary, this woman would also worry about her healthy children as they approached their late teens and early twenties—the time when the symptoms of paranoid schizophrenia frequently appear.

I myself sometimes question whether I'm going crazy. But I take comfort from that old saying that if you're sane enough to ask if you're crazy, you probably aren't.

# Family Escapes

**W**ouldn't it be great if there were emergency exits from our families when times just got too tough? In fact, there are. By the time my brother Frank turned seventeen, he'd saved enough to buy a new car, and handed the money to my parents for safekeeping. When he asked for the money back, my father explained they'd spent it all on bills. Frank was crushed. Unable to deal with our family any longer, he ran down and enlisted in the marines. Because he was still a minor, he had to get my parents to sign the enlistment notice. He told them that if they didn't sign, they'd never see him again. So they signed.

It's ironic that my brother chose the same way to flee his family as my father had decades earlier—by joining the military. My dad, tired of being a farmhand for his foster family, had run away and joined the army. Like my brother Frank, he was also underage.

Each family has its acceptable and unacceptable way of getting out. Why do you think most kids are so excited to go to college? It gets them away from the folks. Not that we don't love them. But even George W.'s twin daughters preferred spring break in Cancún to heading back to the White House for the holidays. Of course, when college isn't an option, some girls "get out" the time-honored way—by getting pregnant. Then there's the "bad marriage" phenomenon. You know what I'm referring to, where the girl has been dating a guy all through high school just so she can get out of the house. She marries the guy, but somehow, once they're hitched, all the problems she thought she was leaving behind get dragged into her *new* house.

Showbiz is also a great family escape. It's club that has its own rules. Once you're in, there's a certain degree of acceptance—at least from those on the outside imagining how glamorous it is inside. It's like getting into that college you always dreamed about.

If I had it in my power, I'd create a flight-attendant-like person who'd stop by certain houses periodically and point out where the emergency exits are located. When a plane is about to take off, attendants remind passengers that if the cabin is losing oxygen, adults should put on their masks so they can help the kids with theirs. That's pretty good advice. Parents need to get *their* act together or they won't be effective in giving their kids what they truly need.

To carry the plane metaphor a bit further, I was once told that a 747 steers itself by constantly adjusting to being off course. It's never actually *on* course, but somehow gets to its destination anyway. To me, healthy families work the same way. They realize there's no "perfect" course, and even if there were, they'd find it impossible to stick to it. Rather, they just constantly try to stay aware of their position.

# Family Humor

I was working on this book on a plane when a young man seated next to me, who happened to have read my previous books, asked me to include a chapter on family humor. Humor has been so intrinsic to my family's way of dealing with things that I almost forgot it. I asked the young man, Dave, how humor had played a role in his family.

He hesitated, then confessed that once his sister had superglued her eyes shut. Apparently, she was using some glue to apply fake fingernails and rubbed her eyes, which caused her eyelids to get stuck. Her whole family went with her to the emergency room, and they never let her forget it.

Good-natured teasing and funny stories told around the dinner table can help bond a family. My dad, for example, would crack a joke and then someone would try to one-up him, followed by someone else trying to do the same thing. We'd often end up in tears, laughing.

I pried further into Dave's life and he confessed that at his house, when the phone rings during dinner, people sometimes joke that "It's Dave's girlfriend." Although twenty-five, a nice guy, and successful enough to fly in first class, he hasn't yet had much luck with the ladies. It appears to be a case of Nice Guy Syndrome, a situation where Dave hasn't yet learned to project the aloofness that attracts many women (possibly because aloofness was a quality exhibited by their fathers).

It seems to me that jokes do three things that are important: 1) they acknowledge what's really going on in families, 2) they offer acceptance (Dave has no girlfriend, but we can talk about it; Sis is such a spaz that she superglued her eyes shut—but she's *our* spaz so it's okay), and 3) they release tension that would otherwise be there when tricky subjects come up for discussion.

Each family has its own humor. Despite all the trouble I experienced in my family, I can remember hysterical laughter being a frequent part of our lives. I call it "dysfunctional humor." Like, there were certain jokes that only *we* understood. Here's an example: Once a month a welfare worker would visit our home. We received $53 a month (in those days, about enough to pay for rent in the projects) to supplement the family income, and the worker was there to make sure we weren't living too high on the hog, that we still were vitally in need of that $53.

It was considered taboo, for instance, to have too new a car or other things that were considered luxury items, like a color TV. But because of my mother's resourcefulness at garage sales and my dad's ability to fix things, we managed to have a color set—an old Magnavox. The color part of it was that the picture showed different shades of green.

So every time this welfare worker was coming, we had to hide the Magnavox, because if we were caught with something like that, they'd force us to sell it and live off the money. The trouble was, once the TV was removed, a big space was created in the living room. So my mom would position four or five of us kids in front of the space. The woman would show up, and my mom would offer her coffee and something to eat, which she always declined. She'd question my dad about how work was going, and my mom about any money coming in. It was an interrogation.

Even though I was young, I understood how much my dad resented this. And yet it was always amazing to see how charming he could be when forced to be on his best behavior. This woman would stay forty-five minutes to an hour and finally my dad would see her out. After he'd shut the door, he'd turn to my mom and say sarcastically, "Isn't she a *wonderful* woman? We should get her a gift. I'd like to get her a beautiful razor-blade necklace."

And then we'd all break up in hysterical laughter. I mean, people were *drooling*. Mom couldn't breathe. Even Dad would be laughing so hard he'd almost cough his false teeth out. To some, this might seem harsh and cruel and a little psycho. But it was our family's humor and it helped us survive.

## FAMILY SURVIVAL TIP

### (for all you jokers)

**#44 Remember to laugh.** Sometimes we get so serious about family issues, we forget to laugh. When times are dark, it's okay to take out the whoopee cushion.

# Functional Families

Because of my background, I'm sometimes reluctant to speak about functional families. Partly, it's because I tend to confuse them with "perfect families"—those households where everyone supposedly has no problems and everything runs smoothly. But one of the blessings of working on this book has been that my consciousness has been expanded by the people I've questioned. Thanks to these folks, I'm beginning to get a sense of what a functional family might look like.

Perhaps my first clue about what a hot-button issue this had become for me came when I was in a restaurant with a group of people, discussing the various problems they'd experienced in their families. When I turned to one young woman who'd been quiet and asked about her family, she simply told me they were great. There was no ambivalence there. I pressed her and she said there was nothing more to say. She loved her relatives and spoke with them every day. They were "great"—end of story.

When I mentioned that I'd been asking these sorts of questions wherever I went and that it was rare for someone to say that their family didn't have at least a few "issues," she theorized that people from dysfunctional families probably feel a greater need to talk about them. Those for whom family life is a struggle tend to vent; those for whom it is placid tend to talk about other things.

At first, I was suspicious. Okay, *very* suspicious. But as I watched her enjoying the rest of the evening with her friends, having fun, being in the moment, I was able to accept that maybe she *did* have a good relationship with her family, and for that reason lacked the desire I'd seen in so many to connect with what was missing in their upbringing. It occurred to me that, if I had a daughter, I'd want her to talk things over with me and not some stranger in a restaurant.

Still, I was unsure. No one knows what *really* goes on behind closed doors—as has been repeatedly proven over the last decade with the O.J. trial, Bill Clinton and Monica, and the Enron debacle. Politicians and religious leaders who promote family values have too often shown themselves to be frauds and hypocrites. Actors who've portrayed sweet and loving family figures have later appeared in the pages of *People* magazine, apologizing for a wide variety of family screwups. In short, this is a world where what we see on the surface frequently doesn't match what's underneath.

But I *have* witnessed moments that make me think I should give tales of family harmony more credit. I was talking on the phone with my friend Larry when suddenly he tossed the phone to his wife Phyllis and started playfully wrestling with two of his sons. I could hear the laughter, and even through the telephone line feel what could only be described as love. Having dinner at their house the next week, I mentioned to Larry and Phyllis that they seemed to have a great family. Modestly, they suggested other families they knew who were truly "great." But even *they* were curious whether any household could hold up under close inspection. They admitted they worked *hard* to make their home as warm a place as possible. And they considered themselves lucky.

My musing about apparently functional families eventually led to thoughts of my friends John and Susan. When John took this book's family I.Q. test, his answers—save for one—indicated impeccable family health. The exception was the answer to "How *truthful* is your family?" John said "pretty" rather than "very." Right there, I had grounds to discount everything he said, but something told me not to.

John's come up before in this book as the motorcycle riding Outlaw-in-Law who eventually became a beloved member of his in-law's family. Both he and Susan were the black sheep of the households they grew up in. Perhaps because of this they had to find their own way. Over the subsequent forty years of their marriage, they've spoken to each other countless times on the phone during the day. Some of their friends have even accused them of being *too* dependent on each other. At the beginning of the marriage, they had few common interests. He loved to race cars; she loved to write stories. She came from an upscale, wealthy, cultured background; he was a blue-collar kid from the streets. But as the years passed, they developed things to do together. They both learned to play tennis, and then in later years, bridge. They went on diets together and took trips to places neither had been before. But mostly they were parents together of three children—who, by the way, all live within ten miles of them. All three kids are seemingly happily married with kids of their own.

Like I said, I could have dismissed John's glowing responses about his family as not being a 100 percent

truthful. But recently I got the chance to watch John play with one of his many grandchildren—Carter—a forty-pound two-year-old who looks like he could join the WWF in a couple years. And watching the two interact, with other family members looking on in appreciation, I thought, well, how can you *deny* the good feelings here, the lack of even slight tension.

John will be the first to tell you his family isn't perfect. But they work at being as supportive of each other as they can. They talk to one another. They try to figure things out.

I've been thinking about the phrase "functional family" and I realize it's just that. A family that functions. It doesn't have to be like families on TV. It doesn't have to be without problems.

In considering functional families, it should also be kept in mind that even *dys*functional families have their functional moments. It's important to hold on to those—to build on them when it's your turn to create your own family.

# Family Directions

**R**ecently, I stayed at a hotel in a major metropolitan area. At the end of my stay, I asked a member of the hotel staff how to get to the airport. Here are the directions I received:

> Go North on I–35 2.3 miles then turn left .4 miles, turn slight right, merge onto South U.S. 81 S, take exit number 237A toward Airport Blvd. Take 38A half a street, take the ramp toward north Airport Blvd., keep right at fork of ramp for .2 miles, keep left at the fork of the ramp for .3 miles. Veer onto Airport Blvd. Take the 111 loop, turn slight left, then turn slight right onto Presidential Blvd. . . .

There's one direction they left out: "Pull over to the shoulder, get out of the car, and start crying." These directions had obviously been obtained from a Web site. For me, all this techno-babble just doesn't translate. Go down the road 2.3 miles? A line like that makes me wish I'd paid closer attention in math class. Sure, I know how far a mile is. As a kid, I had to walk that far and farther a few times. But *driving* a mile? Well, okay, I could use

Why do I and so many other people have trouble remembering directions? My theory is that it has to do with listening. Sometimes it's hard to hear what other people are saying. And like so many other things, it has to do with how we're brought up. From the time we start walking and talking, we're constantly being steered and veered, told where we can and can't go.

I wonder if that's why I often have trouble accepting the directions I'm given. There's some stubbornness in me that turns my brain off when people are telling me what to do, where to go. Even though sometimes I'm the one who asked for directions in the first place, I just feel compelled to go out and find that place by myself. In the Anderson family, even if we go the wrong way, we'd rather pretend we're where we intended than admit we're lost.

If you watch a couple driving somewhere whose location they're not sure of, you'll see this listening dynamic in action. Many comedians have gotten mileage out of the fact that a man is traditionally reluctant to ask for directions while a woman will immediately pull over at the first sign of trouble. But a couple I know exhibits reverse behavior. Wendy and Richard were meeting me at a gig in Cleveland, driving from Pittsburgh. It's usually a two-hour drive, and about two-and-a-half hours into the trip Richard sensed they were lost and suggested they pull over and ask someone. But Wendy insisted they were fine, that there was no way they could miss a whole city. An hour later, they found themselves in a gas station in Elyria listening to a local tell them the bad news: They'd overshot their destination by an hour and were almost out of the state.

It's all about communication, isn't it? This same couple told me an interesting story about a time they the odometer to gauge it, but one wonders how many accidents have been caused by people trying to squint at those tiny digits scrolling by while simultaneously keeping their eyes on the road. Too many, I'll bet.

And getting human directions isn't always the answer either. I used to do a routine about being on the road and pulling into a gas station to ask for directions.

*First off, the dumbest guy in town is the guy who has the job at the gas station. And you know you're in trouble when he starts repeating everything you say.*

*"Excuse me, sir. Do you know where the college is?"*

*"Uh, um, the college . . . ?"*

*You're in real trouble when he looks down at the ground. You know why he's looking down at the ground? Because he dropped his brain down there.*

*"Uh, I was just here looking for my brain. If you help me put it back in my head, I can tell ya . . ."*

*Then you spot another guy hanging out and go ask him.*

*"Oh, uh, I'm just here helping him look for his brain."*

*Finally, an old man pulls into the station. You can usually trust an old man in these situations—only sometimes he treats you like you've lived in this town your whole life.*

*"Oh, sure. Just go up here to that big building—the only big barn thing, then hang a left when you hit Mrs. Johnson's place . . ."*

*Just give me directions according to food places. Left at the Wendy's. Right at the Hardee's. Stop at the rib place and then turn toward the Oriental Buffet. That I can remember.*

went to see a therapist. After asking several questions, the therapist told them that, according to his rating system, Richard was a "three" and Wendy was a "seven," meaning they were totally incompatible. But then he said something worthwhile. He told Richard that he needed to use fewer words when talking to his wife; and he told Wendy that she needed to use *more* words when talking to her husband. It seems that Richard had been primarily raised by his single mother who'd encouraged him to be highly verbal, so he was used to discussing everything. Conversely, Wendy growing up had strongly identified with her father, who spoke mostly through his actions, so she was most comfortable with silent shorthand. The therapist's advice was solid. We all need to hone the way we say things so the person we're trying to get through to can hear.

# Family Pets

**J**ust as pets often *do* look like their owners, they're often representative of the family they're in. Given that, you might ask why I decided to get two miniature Doberman pinschers. (Note to dog lovers: While they look like Dobermans who have been shrunken in the washing machine, the actual breed is called miniature pinschers, and they are not related to Dobermans.) Part of what attracted me to these dogs was their temperament: These dogs are extremely loyal, which I like to think is one of my best qualities. Part of it is that I sometimes see myself as being physically like them: small, but wiry. I know that sounds odd—*very* odd, considering my girth—but I was the tenth of eleven siblings, so I've always thought of myself as "the little guy."

At first I was thinking about getting a pug, but I'd heard they can have breathing problems. So instead I wound up getting the same type of dog as my sister Tina. I'd developed an attachment to her miniature pinscher Duchess when Tina would bring her along on visits. Growing up, we never really had pets and I could see the affection she had for that little dog.

To get the puppies, I drove out to a breeder in San Bernardino where I had to pick among the litter. It's a

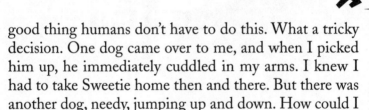

good thing humans don't have to do this. What a tricky decision. One dog came over to me, and when I picked him up, he immediately cuddled in my arms. I knew I had to take Sweetie home then and there. But there was another dog, needy, jumping up and down. How could I ignore Nico?

The problem is, once I got them home, this behavior continued. As I'd approach the fenced-in area in the living room, which I'd set up as their domain, Sweetie would be sweetly affectionate. Nico would be hyper. So naturally, I was more inclined to pick up Sweetie. She was such a docile dog, and would lay happily with me on my bed for hours. Nico, though, would jump around continuously, and after a while, I'd have to put him back in his living quarters. The more I did this, the more jealous, insecure, and rambunctious he became and the less I'd pick him up.

Thus, a deep-seated sibling rivalry was born. How the heck do *any* parents do this right?

Getting the dogs was a big commitment for me. But when I come home, they're there waiting with unconditional love. Isn't that what we all want from our families?

# Fan Mail

*My dad wasn't an alcoholic, he was just mean. We weren't eleven kids, only four. We weren't poor, only lower-middle class. . . . But I know how much the "F" word—"family"—can hurt you and I thank you for sharing your experiences with me.*

—FROM A READER OF *DEAR DAD*

After writing *Dear Dad*, I received thousands of letters from people who identified with the struggles I described in the book. At the time, I was overwhelmed by the number and content of the letters. Often, I couldn't finish them because of their sadness. Other times, though, they made me feel less alone. Mostly, the letters made me realize I'd led a considerably easier life than many people. The snowstorm you're in always seems like the worst snowstorm imaginable—or something like that. I kept all of those letters with the intent of answering them. But you know how good intentions get waylaid.

Recently, I've begun reading the letters again, and as I do I can't help wonder how the lives of those who wrote them have changed. How have their family situations altered in the twelve years since that book was published?

Whether it was the woman who struggled with her weight who'd only written me, Erma Bombeck, and the Pope; or the girl whose partying alcoholic father married five times, and who "managed not to get pregnant till she was sixteen"; or the adult survivor of childhood sexual abuse at the hands of three family members. The writers of those letters amazed me with what they'd lived through and with how hard they'd tried to change. Does time heal? Does therapy help? Do families really change? How?

Lord knows, it's not easy creating a different life than the one you were brought up with.

In fact, while working on *this* book, it seems like an unusual number of people have approached me on the street and mentioned the impact my first book had on them. From what they've shared in these brief encounters, they seemed to be doing okay, having dealt with the demons they were facing. If you believe in signs, then maybe they were telling me something.

To those of you who wrote me before, this is my fan letter to you. It's meant a lot to know you're out there.

## FAMILY SURVIVAL TIP

### (for those with unresolved issues)

**#45 The write thing to do.** Writing letters to my departed father helped me resolve many issues. I really believe in this technique as a means of getting at what's bothering you. On a plane recently I sat next to a young father who was in the military. Because of his base assignment, Norm had spent the past few months away from his two-year-old son, Shawn. To make up for it, Norm wrote to Shawn every day in a journal. Norm wanted to tell his son how he saw life so Shawn could be more connected to him than Norm's father had been to him. In writing down his thoughts, Norm discovered how angry he was at his dad, who all while Norm was growing up had been consumed with running a successful landscaping business, and was rarely home. Prior to keeping the journal, Norm had told himself he understood why his father hadn't been there for him. But when he started to write, he got in touch with his heart, which contained his *real* feelings. That made him more empathetic toward Shawn, who, even at two, might be hurt that his dad wasn't there. I got off that plane convinced Norm was on his way to becoming a great father.

# Family Lost and Found

You're never prepared for loss, especially the loss of someone in your family or someone close. When several years ago one of my good friends called me with the news that her son had been seriously injured in a freak skiing accident, I asked no questions, simply told her I was on my way. I hopped on a plane and headed to Minnesota. On my arrival, I was informed that my friend's son was brain dead.

My friend was so scared and didn't know what to do. You see, her son was on life support and she was being encouraged to take him off so his organs could be used for others. The longer he stayed on life support, the less useful his organs would become. The organ donor people were relentless, putting more pressure on my friend than I felt was warranted. I went to them and told them to get the hell out of the room or we'd sue them for a billion dollars. Not my most tactful moment, admittedly, but when you care about someone, the emotions take over.

After the donor people had exited, I told my friend that if she wanted to leave her son on life support forever, that was okay. I said this because we all need a certain amount of time to deal with loss—*and* because I believe in miracles. An hour after the donor people left, my friend made peace with the idea of letting her son go. She directed that the equipment be disconnected, and her son soon passed.

It always seems grossly unfair when a parent has to bury one of their children. I knew that my friend would be dealing with the loss for some time. And for the next six months, I tried to stay in close contact. Her spirits were very low and I feared for her life. The truth is, I didn't know *what* to do.

Then one day I was watching a TV show and a couple was talking about their son's suicide. On the show was a psychic, a person who claimed to be able to contact people who've passed to the other side. I was skeptical, but something about this guy seemed authentic, and after he contacted the couple's son, they seemed somewhat relieved. I wondered if this psychic could help my friend. I called and told my friend about him. She phoned him and set up a private meeting. After the meeting, she called me and just from her voice, I could tell her grief had been lifted. To my surprise, as a gift, she'd arranged a session for me.

To be honest, I wasn't sure I wanted one. But I *was* curious about this psychic so I went. He was very nice, unassuming, and down to earth. I'd brought a pen and paper to take notes. However, right from the start the session unfolded differently from what I'd expected. Rather than go over my background in detail, the man asked that I reply "yes" or "no" to a few specific questions. Then something seemed to click into place and he began talking:

"There's a woman here who's very excited to see you," he said. "She says she's your mother and the first thing she wants me to tell you is to stop punishing yourself, to stop thinking you didn't do enough for her. She says she wants you to watch where you're walking and be careful of your right knee. She's trying to tell me her name. She keeps pointing to the light around her head. She says I'll never guess it. She has great news about your career. In May, you'll win an award and you'll be changing your career from comedy to drama. Your sister has liver trouble. You'll reconcile with your older brother. She says your dad is here, but still struggling with being here. He's sorry he wasn't a better father, but is very proud of you. She says it's important you keep making people feel better."

The psychic went on to say that I had four or five guardian angels, brothers or sisters, who'd passed over. Up to that point, he'd held my interest, but the last comment about guardian angels sowed some doubt since all my siblings were still alive at the time. I told him this, but he couldn't be dissuaded. "They've always been with you and are excited to talk to you," he said. Then he asked me if my mom had had any stillborn babies. I said "yes": two sets of twins and my parent's first baby. I was stunned because I'd never mentioned this to anyone. I looked down at the pen and paper I'd brought to take notes with and realized I'd written nothing.

After this meeting, I felt numb. Whether this man had really connected with "the other side," who knows? All I can say is, it *felt* real. And the way the ensuing weeks and months seemed to substantiate the things he'd said only made it more so.

Some of the things the psychic had said I knew to be true the day I met with him. It was correct, for example, that since my mother had died, I'd wondered if I'd done enough for her. As for the reference to my leg, I fell onstage and injured my right leg. The light around one's head is called an "aura" and my mother's name was Ora. As for what would happen later, in May of that year, I won my first two Emmys for *Life with Louie*. My sister came down with liver cancer and eventually died before she could get a transplant. My older brother and I eventually reconciled and are now very close.

Could this psychic have done a little research and discovered things like my mother's name, even gone into public records and learned about the stillborn children? Hard to believe he'd do that much preparation in advance, but I suppose. Were some of his predictions more a matter of logical guesswork than access to the spirit world? Perhaps. But so much of what he had to say was on target that I became a believer.

Ultimately, what I may have witnessed that day was a psychic's ability to read a person's unconscious thoughts and help him connect with them. Even if that's all this psychic was capable of, I'd still say it's a pretty rare skill. As things developed, I became friends with this man and introduced him to other celebrities. They seemed to benefit from meeting with him. I was impressed enough to think the whole thing might make a good TV show. So I put a tape together and presented it to the networks. They didn't buy it since there was a show in production called *Crossing Over with John Edwards* (who is *not* the psychic in this story).

The reason I was interested in producing a show like this is because, whether a person can really cross over to "the other side" or not, the hope a psychic like this can give to people *is* real. There's always a need for more hope.

Myself, I choose to believe that some people are able to contact people on the other side for one very good reason: I *want* to believe it.

# Family Pictures/Family Evidence

A friend of mine who I've mentioned previously in this book, Kurt, told me the story of a time when he was thirty-five and sitting with his father in his dad's Oldsmobile outside a Chinese restaurant. They were having the latest in a long series of arguments.

Kurt and his dad had endured an often contentious relationship largely because his father hadn't been there as much as Kurt would have liked after his parents had divorced thirty years earlier. The father, a busy attorney with a second family, contended that his son's childhood hadn't been as painful as his son maintained, despite constant parental skirmishes in which the kids were frequently used as pawns. As proof of his son's *happy* childhood, the father produced a scrapbook showing picture after picture of Kurt and his two brothers smiling—on family vacations, in the backyard, at various graduations.

Kurt pointed out that his father had insisted on having his children "say cheese" before each photo and that these images merely captured a superficial reality. There'd been no photography going on during the battles over who was going to pay for summer camp, or at the baseball games when Kurt had looked forlornly into the seats for a father who never showed up.

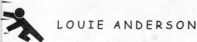
Kurt's dad sadly put the scrapbook back under the seat. Another stalemate.

I used to collect scrapbooks of other people's families that I'd find in flea markets and antique stores. I enjoyed making guesses about what a particular family was like, based on the photos they'd taken. I wonder what strangers would think if they looked at the Anderson family album. *Just another normal Midwestern brood.*

The reality, of course, is that pictures don't always tell the story.

# Family Vacations

**Y**ou're going on a family vacation with your husband and three-year-old daughter to Disney World—"the happiest place on Earth," a place where family fantasy and family reality merge. You've been to Disney World as a little girl and have only the fondest of memories. What could possibly go wrong?

Your friends have told you should really stay at one of the hotels located on the Monorail (to easily get in and out of the park). Also on the list of "must do's": the Princess Character Breakfast where your daughter can have pancakes with Cinderella herself. You share these tips with your husband, who nods and points out that his mother lives in Palm Beach—why not let *her* make the reservations so you can get that Florida resident discount?

Unfortunately, your mother-in-law books a hotel that *isn't* located on the Monorail (because it's cheaper). She also gives Cinderella the heave-ho in favor of Winnie the Pooh. Still, you're determined to not let this faze you.

You arrive at the Magic Kingdom only to discover that the Florida resident discount applies *only* to your mother-in-law and the whole trip would have been cheaper had your husband let you book it through Triple A like you wanted to. As you all pile onto the tram, your husband and Grandma blissfully discuss with your daughter the different Disney characters that mark each parking row. Meanwhile, you trail behind, clutching a hard-to-fold stroller, a heavy diaper bag, and three cameras your husband insisted on bringing.

You enter the Magic Kingdom with a plan of how to divide the time so that the four of you can see everything. You're going to start at Toon Town and work your way clockwise. But your husband sees a few people lining up on Main Street for the Dreams Come True parade, and though you've spent all morning getting here and are only a few feet into the park, he insists on waiting right where you are. So your first hour is spent sitting on a curb, jockeying for position with other parents.

At one point someone knocks over a Slurpee and your daughter becomes transfixed by the ants crawling all over it. Who needs a parade to enthrall this young one? Finally, Mickey appears in a glass bubble—looking somewhat like the Pope when he travels in his Popemobile. Peter Pan comes by on a float and tells everyone, "Don't close your eyes, we're just getting started." As the Princesses pass—Sleeping Beauty, Cinderella, Belle, and Ariel—your daughter asks when she's going to have breakfast with all of them. Feeling guilty, you put on a cheery voice and tell her you have an even *better* treat for her: She's going to have dinner with Pooh. She proceeds to throw a tantrum, crying for Cinderella and trying to run after the float.

The parade ends and you try not to worry about falling behind schedule. Your husband passes the Dumbo flying elephant ride and insists the line doesn't look *that* long. Why not give it a whirl? He fails to see the way the line twists and turns, and it's an hour before you finally get to the front of the line. That's when your daughter insists she has to go the bathroom. Your mother-in-law takes her as you and your husband ride on Dumbo, feeling somewhat foolish.

That night, feet aching, bone tired, you think about the afternoon, but the only images that come to mind are of all those gift shops you passed through at the end of each attraction. As you empty your purse of receipts, it occurs to you that Disney World is kind of like Las Vegas for kids. The gift shops vacuum up your money as efficiently as any casino.

Even so, you still regret *not* buying that Princess gown—with matching glass slippers and tiara—that your daughter fell in love with midway through the afternoon. Your husband saw the price tag and his reaction was the same as your father's all those years ago. Absolutely "no way" was he paying that much for a dress he could get "for a third the price" outside the gates.

The next day, you do it all again, slugging your way through Fantasy Land, Tomorrow Land, Frontier Land, and *Exhaustion* Land. Each member of the family takes a turn getting lost and by late afternoon your daughter is covered in cotton candy, her new white sweater, bought especially for this occasion, is irreparably stained.

Spirits soar when a rumor circulates that Cinderella is inside the lobby of the Royal Table Restaurant signing autographs. You grab your daughter and head toward the entryway where the hostess puts a body block on you, pointing out that only restaurant patrons are allowed inside. Your daughter's heartfelt pleadings do nothing to persuade her. As your mother-in-law wades

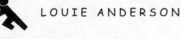
into the battle, your husband seizes on the hostess's temporary distraction and sneaks your daughter into the restaurant. You slip in a few minutes later.

There she is, Cinderella herself. Your daughter is finally face-to-face with royalty, her dreams come true. And what does she do? Totally freezes, holding tightly to your husband's leg. Cinderella signs her autograph book and smiles. As your daughter is about to leave, she stops to curtsy just like she practiced at home. Your heart skips a beat.

Seeing that even your husband is touched by the encounter, you decide to renew the push for a princess gown purchase. He says you're being insensitive about how much this trip has already cost, pointing out that nothing is ever enough. You shoot back that the whole trip would have cost a lot less if he'd let *you* book it instead of his mother. He accuses you of not appreciating all his mother has done. You accuse him of not appreciating all *you've* done. Suddenly, even though you're in "the happiest place on Earth," you're not speaking to each other.

Your mother-in-law informs you that a show with all the Disney characters is about to start in front of the castle. Grudgingly, you head over and watch as Snow White, Prince Charming, the genie from *Aladdin*, and Mickey Mouse all sing that the really important gifts in life *aren't* material things, but what's in your heart. Your husband gives you a look, suggesting you haven't yet absorbed this profound message.

Of course, you're not about to give him the satisfaction of conceding he might be right. He's just using Disney characters to justify his cheapness.

After the performance, your daughter insists on waiting with the masses for a chance to meet Mickey, who like a president running for reelection is standing with his handlers behind a rope, shaking hands. It's finally your daughter's turn when another couple pushes in front with their five-year-old daughter and Mickey spends what seems like an inordinate amount of time hugging her. The little girl's mother leans in to take photographs and you're about to comment on the delay when suddenly Mickey points to the pink button on the five-year-old's dress. You're wondering about the significant of the button when the little girl's mother turns to you and says "Thanks." She adds that her daughter is on a Make-A-Wish trip and has leukemia.

Your daughter meets Mickey and your husband gets a picture. As you move away from the crowd, you apologize to him for being so silly about that expensive dress. He tells you that he feels bad himself and insists on going back and getting it. You tell him he doesn't really need to. Your mother-in-law offers to solve the whole problem by paying for the dress herself. You thank her sincerely.

As your daughter walks out of the park wearing her white Cinderella gown and tiara, people stop and tell you what a beautiful princess she makes. Suddenly, in the skies above the castle, fireworks go off and it's as if Walt Disney himself had choreographed the moment.

On the way home, your husband asks your daughter what she liked best about her visit to the Magic Kingdom. She mentions that Slurpee with the ants crawling over it. You and your husband laugh. You realize how much pressure you'd put on yourself to have a perfect time and how little it all mattered. Your daughter would probably have been just as happy to go to Cardboard Box Kingdom where she could play with those foam peanuts they use for packaging.

You think back to your own trip to Disneyland when you were a kid and suddenly recall that your father was always stressed about how much money was being spent, your mother was always worried about you getting sunburned, and you and your brother argued incessantly about which ride to go on. As you put your little princess to bed that night, an image comes to you of the Make-A-Wish girl. Suddenly, you give your daughter a long hug and plant a kiss on your husband's cheek. The next time you go on vacation, you vow not to worry so much about the little things.

## FAMILY SURVIVAL TIP

### (for going on a trip)

**#46 Dare to be different.** Next family vacation, think about choosing a place where none of you have been before—and might not normally go. Make it an adventure for each of you. Maybe you'll discover something as a family.

# Family Holidays

How was your last Thanksgiving? That's my favorite holiday. That's my mom's favorite holiday because she always gets to invite the aunt and uncle everybody hates. And I know this by what my dad says when he walks out of the bedroom and sees them.

[Giving my dad's stare.] "Oh boy. I'll be in the garage."

My aunt and uncle never bring anything except that tub of lime-green Jell-O with the shredded carrots mixed in. What, did their aquarium freeze up? My mom always makes too much food. Like one item especially. Six or seven hundred pounds of sweet potatoes. So she's got to push it during the meal.

[Imitating Mom.] "Did you get the sweet potatoes? There are sweet potatoes. They're hot. There are some in the oven. There are more in the garage . . ."

I know I'll be seeing this stuff for months later.

"Hey, Mom, what's this orange stuff in the tuna fish?"

"Oh, that's just something I'm trying."

My dad can only take my mom's pushing of sweet potatoes so long.

"Shut up! Gimme some of those."

*Then my mother can't help but chime in: "Did you get a hot biscuit? There are hot biscuits."*

*Has it ever happened that you finish the meal, you're eating the dessert and all of a sudden your mom stands up and says, "The cranberries!"*
*She looks at you with urgency.*
*"Get them. They're on the bottom shelf."*

*You know you're getting older when the first thing you're thinking about after the meal is finding a place to lie down. My mom would always wait till my dad got real nice and comfortable and then she'd get him.*
*"Could you take them home?"*
*My dad would look over at the relatives he never wanted to invite in the first place.*
*"Louie, come with me so I don't hurt them."*
*He'd be mean to them too. He'd ask them horrible questions.*
*"Your son get out of prison yet?"*
*I'd try to stop him: "Da-a-d!"*
*Well, he'd try to apologize to them, but it just wouldn't be in him.*
*"Uh, eh . . ." he'd mumble as the relatives got out of the car. But he just couldn't do it.*
*They'd get inside the house and he'd tell me, "Go ahead, throw that Jell-O on the lawn."*

While writing this book, I journeyed to the Minneapolis area, where my family is located, for the Christmas holiday. Don't you hate packing for a trip? As much luggage as I own, I still don't feel I have the right pieces, especially for a thirteen-day trip. Fifteen pairs of socks, fifteen T-shirts, fifteen pairs of boxers, toiletries, casual clothes, two suits, shoes—and already the bag is full. At least for me, there's always the temptation to say forget it—I'm not going. What *is* this queasy feeling some of us get when we start to head home for Christmas?

Maybe it's that we've just finished eating Thanksgiving dinner with these people last month and now, before we even have time to digest the turkey, we have to go back and give everyone gifts. Sometimes, don't you just want to wrap up that turkey carcass and hand it to them? Why can't we just move Thanksgiving to August? Then at least we'd have four months to recover. I sometimes think the reason people drink on New Year's is not to celebrate the new year, but to congratulate themselves for getting through the holidays alive.

Luckily, this year I didn't have to pack gifts. I'd already sent my brothers and sisters money. That might sound impersonal, but the truth is, despite all I've gone through, I still do have a somewhat impersonal relationship with my family. I've really worked hard on making my relationship with them better, and I hoped this trip to Minneapolis would be a turning point.

The suitcase nearly didn't squeeze shut—no matter how much I put in there, a final tug is always required. It doesn't matter if I take two shirts or twelve bowling balls—it always won't close by half an inch. As I sat on the suitcase, I looked up at the TV and there was Martha Stewart giving tips on how to make Christmas brighter. Just once I'd like her to do a show that deals with what many *real* families go through:

*Today on Martha Stewart's Dysfunctional Family Christmas Special, I'll show you how to transform your brother's parole papers into a lovely snowflake. With a little ribbon, we'll learn how to turn Dad's old whiskey bottles into delightful tree ornaments. And we'll convert that broken lamp your uncle Ernie threw at Aunt Phyllis during Thanksgiving into a festive centerpiece.*

As I arrived at the L.A. airport, I was reminded of how many people travel for Christmas. There were hoards of moms, dads, and kids crowding the terminal. Were these families anything like mine? Looking around, I saw what I imagined were young actresses going back to where they'd have to worry about playing a different part, fiancés on their way to meet prospective in-laws, and businessmen who probably have no problem performing the hard sell but dread facing their aging parents.

I finally got to the counter and was told, first, that I'd been flagged to be searched an extra time at the gate, and second, that my flight had been delayed two hours. Am I the only one who suspects the airline uses this ploy when they have an underbooked flight and want to economize by combining two in one?

*Two* hours. Well, at least I can smoke, I thought. But hadn't I smoked enough? The line to get to the security check-in was already out the door. Even before 9/11, I never felt secure with airport security people. I always wanted to help them by pointing out someone in line and saying, "Check that guy—I saw him in my spy pamphlet." But whenever I was tempted, they'd be busy with some cowboy from Texas who'd be explaining, "Uh, gee, must be my buckle."

I thought about the widely reported story of the passenger who was caught with bombs hidden in his shoes. I wondered what he was thinking as he walked through the airport: "Geez, hope these things don't explode."

As the security people waved their wand around my frame and searched through my stuff, a couple people nearby recognized me. "Hey, *Feud* guy . . ." "Dude, survey says . . ."

Weirdly, a list came to mind, "Things You'd Find In a Comedian-Gameshow Host's Suitcase": *Four rubber chickens, two thousand autographed headshots, a voodoo doll of that* Weakest Link *lady. A dozen Krispy Kreme donuts.* Okay, the donuts have nothing to do with comedy or gameshows, but there's no way I was going to survive on those tiny bags of peanuts the airlines give you.

I own all this expensive luggage, but still it was a shopping bag I brought onboard the plane. It was exactly what my mother used to carry onboard. Yes, she's no longer alive, but she's still always with *us*—her eleven kids. (Actually, only nine now, since my sister Mary and brother Bill died in the past couple of years.)

I know life is short, so why didn't I feel better about going home to see my family?

The security guard informed me that I had two lighters, which isn't allowed. I guess one lighter is okay, but two, in the wrong hands, can be turned into a nuclear device. For a moment, I was secretly relieved at the prospect of *not* having to get on that plane. So what if they arrested me. In a way, I'd just be trading one jail for another.

Don't the holidays sometimes feel like jail—family jail? Instead of bread and water, you get bread, bread, bread, turkey, turkey, turkey, mashed potatoes, mashed potatoes, mashed potatoes, lumpy gravy, lumpy gravy, lumpy gravy, enough, enough, enough already. With all those relatives around, you sometimes find yourself praying for solitary confinement. And this isn't just a yearly event—it's a life sentence. Sometimes you think maybe you should have asked for the gas chamber.

Don't get me wrong. I love my family. I really do. What I have a hard time coping with—and I'm sure *they* feel the same toward me—is being around them for a long period of time. I have to confess, there's a reason I've chosen to work the last six Christmas holidays in Las Vegas. *Work* Christmas? Yes. For me, it's a great way to avoid a lot of bad memories.

Frankly, I think a lot of people would get out of Christmas if they could. (Recently, John Grisham wrote a very well received novel based on that premise.) In fact, when I'm in Vegas for the holiday I open my act by using a conspiratorial tone with the audience, pointing out that they've managed to escape Christmas, too. That usually gets a big laugh of recognition.

This holiday was somewhat unique because I was scheduled to do my annual nonalcoholic New Year's show with Roseanne, whom I'd worked with fifteen years ago just before she became a TV legend. I thought getting together with her might be an interesting exercise in closure. Back when Roseanne's show was rocketing to number one, I'd been offered a television show by the late great Brandon Tartikoff, then the head of NBC. At the last minute, I'd turned it down because of a gut feeling. I'd seen some of the emotional ups and downs Roseanne was contending with as a result of her success, and I felt if I did a TV show at that time, it might kill me.

Whether that was a cop-out for my own insecurities, I still didn't know. But instead of doing that TV show, I went on to write *Dear Dad* and spend time with my mother who died unexpectedly a few years later. The question was still, *Did I take the right path? Have I learned anything by going down this road?*

I landed in Minneapolis and met my friend Carl, who helped me write this book. Carl was expecting me to immediately contact my family. I learned a while ago, though, to limit my time and energy. I had a lot of promotion to do for the show with Roseanne, and used that as an excuse for putting off calling them.

Instead, Carl and I drove to the places where I grew up in St. Paul: the duplex in the projects, the house that Uncle Ike gave my dad the down payment for, the house next to the bowling alley where Dad worked at one point. We passed Ames Elementary School where we had to line up—the normal kids on one side; the projects kids on the other. We even cruised by the metal pole that I convinced my brother Mikey to touch his tongue to in the middle of winter. (That became good material for my act.)

They're still there—all these places from my childhood. I'm still sorting out which parts are fact, fiction, and fantasy. As we drove around in my rented Buick Park Avenue, everything seemed smaller than in my memory. The hill we'd run up. The walk from school that seemed to take forever.

They've redone the projects since we lived there—the Roosevelt Housing Projects. They actually look *nice* now—well, except for a few up the road that remain exactly as they were. Across the way is a building complex the neighborhood kids used to set fire to as it was being constructed. The workers had taken away our woodsy stomping grounds, so every time the guys with hammers got half finished some of the kids would burn down the structure. At least, that's how I remember it. The builders had to hire twenty-four-hour guards. As I turned from looking at the complex, I realized we'd pulled up in front of the duplex where I lived, 1122A Hazelwood.

I stared at the place where I'd gotten so much material for my act, where so much of me was formed, the place where I was born. A woman carrying plastic shopping bags started to head in the door. I rolled down my window and shouted over the passenger seat: "Hi."

"Hi."

"I used to live here."

"What?"

"I used to live here."

"Oh, okay."

What was she supposed to say to that? "Come on in." She must have thought I was planning on robbing her. Carl tried to reassure her by citing my chief credit at the time.

"Have you seen *Family Feud?*"

"Oh yeah," she said nonchalantly with no sign of recognition.

"He's the host."

Now she must have really thought we were crazy. *Yeah, and Bob Barker is in the car behind us.* I leaned across Carl and shouted out through the passenger side window.

"Do you think I could come by and look at it sometime?"

"Sure."

As the woman headed inside unfazed, I realized I probably wouldn't come back. The truth is, I'd stopped by a few years before and a Thai family was living there. I didn't go in then either. Apparently, the Thai family had moved on. People move on from the projects. If they're lucky.

We drove over to the house my parents had lived in after they left the projects, but it didn't mean as much to me. Not as many memories, I guess. Then on over to the Hillcrest Bowl where my dad had his last job. We rented a house right next to it on Hoyt. (By that time, it was just me, Mikey, Dad, and Mom.) We drove by the White Bear Steak House where my dad and I used to get a steak dinner: steak, salad, Texas toast, and drink.

"Don't order that Texas toast. I'll give you mine," my dad would say, trying to save the extra fifteen cents. We'd sit there together, just him and me.

"Eh, friggin' world is something, isn't it, Louie?"

Him and me. Two Louies against the world.

All this sightseeing into the past was making me hungry so we drove by Jerry's Chicken—another place my dad used to take us for a treat. A restaurant where they sent people out to your car to take your order. It's still in business and the chicken tastes as good as it did forty years ago. This stuff is cooked in 750 degree oil with what my brother Kyle claims is beer-flavored batter. Tender, juicy generous portions of white-meat chicken. Food—it can bring the good parts of your childhood back in a second. Is it any wonder I eat? What's better than that?

I ran into a convenience store for a pack of cigarettes and some water, and the kid behind the counter recognized me. He told me who his dad was and it turned out his dad was a friend of mine growing up. He still lived in the neighborhood. I offered the kid and his dad some free tickets for my New Year's show. I wrote down their name on a piece of paper so I could have tickets waiting at the door. But as I told the kid where the concert was, down by the college campus, I knew there wasn't much chance of them showing up. People from the projects usually hang around the projects. It's what's comfortable.

I have to admit, there was something very *comforting* about being back home. The people seemed nicer, more real. I've lived in L.A. twenty years, but, as I've mentioned, most of my real friends are still from Minneapolis. For better or worse, people there are living lives, raising families. They're not worrying about what deal they're going to get next to make them richer or more famous, or what car they'll have to drive to look cool. They're the America a lot of show business people originally come from, the people entertainers are speaking to when they're at their most truthful.

As I tooled around the Twin Cities in the rented Buick, I drove more wildly than I do back in L.A.; I drove like a sixteen-year-old kid who'd just gotten his freedom. I can still remember Dad getting me my first car—a Buick Electra. Even though we were always poor, my father would make sure all us kids owned cars. He'd buy them for fifty bucks and put a couple hundred into fixing them up.

I always wanted to do a one-man show of Dad under his prized Bonneville asking me to hand him his tools. "Louie, give me the three-eighth!" I didn't have a clue what he was talking about. He always had that car jacked up and I'd hand him something only to hear an instant later: "That's not a three-eighth, you lardass!" As he continued yelling, I'd stare at that jack holding the car up and think: "college" or "prison"?

We all got out, somehow. None of my siblings live in the projects. Some live nearby, but basically, we all got out. The girls got out mostly by getting married and getting pregnant—not always in that order. Sometimes they were only fifteen. No one really talked much about birth control back then. And let's face it, my mom, as matriarch to a brood of eleven, wasn't exactly a spokeswoman for contraception.

Unfortunately, most of my sisters wound up picking guys just like dear old Dad. It was a type they recognized: the bad-boy drinker. But, for the most part, they've done their best to raise their kids better and are now proud grandmothers.

Thomas Wolfe wrote that you can't go home again. But I wonder if he realized that most of us never *leave*. Rather, we take home with us in our heads.

Thinking back, I remember daydreaming in the duplex on Hazelwood that maybe I'd be famous one day. Not that I dreamed of being a comedian. I thought I'd be president. Be president and fix all the world's problems. Then maybe I'd get around to fixing my family. Once when I was on *The Tonight Show* I walked over to the band during a break and told Doc Severinsen that he was one of my dad's favorite trumpet players. Then I asked him what a "D-horn" was. My dad used to always call guys he was mad at a D-horn. He'd be behind someone in traffic and yell out, "friggin' D-horn!"

Tommy Newsome, Doc's right-hand man, had the answer. "You can't play the trumpet in the key of D."

So someone who's a D-horn is a guy who has no idea what he's doing. Thanks for the info, Tommy.

Sometimes it's hard to reconcile the two realities: my life as it was and as it has become.

# Family
# Cell-a-brations

*During the holidays, there are all these rituals we go through with our families. One tradition I'll never forget is going to the Christmas tree lot with my dad who was always looking to outsmart the guy selling the trees.*

*"I know how to work these guys, Louie. They buy them for a quarter a piece, by the billions."*

*My mom would pick the tree out.*

*"I'll take this one," she'd say, "but that one looks like it could use a good home . . . or maybe this one that smells so good . . ."*

*Once she'd decided, Dad went to work negotiating.*

*"Hey, buddy, how much for this tree without any limbs?"*

*"Thirty-five dollars."*

*"What?! Are you going to come over and decorate it for us? I'll give you three bucks for it."*

*I'd be mortified. "Oh my God. He's not our legal father!"*

*Then my dad wouldn't pay fifty cents for the rope.*

*"I got the rope in the car."*

*We'd carry the tree over to the station wagon; he'd open the trunk and find nothing.*

*"You kids been taking that rope again?"*

*"Oh yeah, Dad. We wait until you and Mom fall asleep, we get those car keys, we open that trunk, we get that rope—we've got enough in our room to hang the whole neighborhood!"*

*Then we'd end up holding the tree on to the car, our hands freezing in the cold. Once we got the tree home, my dad would make us get the stand from the base-ment—the stand that came over on the* Mayflower.

*"That's a good stand!" he'd bellow. "When I was a kid, we didn't have stands! We had to take turns holding that tree!"*

*He'd get the saw and work on that stand for hours. Finally, we'd put the tree in the stand and inevitably the tree would lean over, crooked. My dad would frown and yell at the tree: "For thirty-five bucks, that thing should dance!"*

*You ever get your dad something that he already had for Christmas? Something he already owned? Some-thing that was his?*

*My dad would open up his present and find one of his tools.*

*"Hey, I was looking all over for this."*

*I'd turn to my brother.*

*"Wait till he looks in that other box and finds all that rope."*

**C**hristmas Day, Carl and I drove through the empty streets of downtown Minneapolis. I took him to the Mall of America—the largest mall in the country, second largest in the world. That's the one with its own amusement park and condos, a brick-and-steel ode to consumerism. On this particular day, it sat quietly, oddly vacant. This was the day when families were home, exchanging gifts. Were they getting what they wanted?

Sometimes, of course, even receiving a nice gift does little to relieve the pressure of being around our family during the holidays. There are all those minefields to negotiate. People are still mad about the sixth-grade incident, the seventh-grade incident, the disappointment of not being able to afford a certain college because Mom and Dad didn't save, the bitterness that derives from Mom's not liking our husband or wife.

Then there's the pressure of the gifts themselves— the illusion that if we get the right gift it will fix everything. That illusion starts becoming part of our mindset when we're told to get on Santa's lap and tell him what we want. A while ago, I saw a series of ads in which adults sit on Santa's lap and are asked what they want. The answer? More time to get their shopping done, for people not to be critical of their gift choices, and a way out of seeing their in-laws.

Someone once told me there are three kinds of gift-givers: those who give gifts to show people what big shots they are; those who give gifts to please—a safe gift; and those—call them "reluctant gift-givers"—who give gifts at the last minute. My advice is this: Give the gift you want to *yourself.* Then you won't put pressure on your loved ones to deliver.

Carl and I eventually went our separate ways for the rest of Christmas, with me spending the holiday alone. (I think it's okay *not* to participate in holidays.) That day, I talked to a security guard at a twenty-four-hour drugstore who told me he was happy to be spending the day working. He'd gotten into a fight with his wife because he'd bought himself a little something for Christmas and his wife had found it and was mad. I told him my theory of how you should buy yourself what you want for Christmas. Then he told me that the gift he'd gotten for himself, which he'd left lying in his closet with the wrapping paper, was an AK-47.

For some reason, this guy's wife wasn't too keen on his spending over a thousand dollars on a machine gun that could spew out fifty rounds at a time. "Of course, that kind of gun is illegal," the guard informed me, "but this one was modified so it only shoots ten rounds at a time." He'd bought it for hunting and couldn't understand why his wife was so upset. After all, he'd bought *her* the vacuum cleaner she wanted.

So much for my great theories.

You can learn a lot by spending the holidays by yourself. Mostly, you learn by noting the absence of things. Not having to pretend how happy you are when you open your gift. Not worrying about saying the wrong thing, which will lead to yet another family fight. You know how people wish for "peace on Earth" during Christmas? If you spend the holiday by yourself, sometimes it can feel that way—like "peace on Earth." At least, to a kid from the projects with an alcoholic father who's spent a lifetime trying to compensate for a lot of disappointing Christmases.

I planned on seeing my family *after* Christmas. Roseanne was coming to town to get ready for the show and I had to make sure she felt welcome. And the firefighters—I had to go by the station house like I promised. After all, we were doing this New Year's show partly as a benefit for them.

I'd never been to a firehouse before and was very

impressed with all these earnest, hard-working people whom we tend to take for granted. I remember when I was a kid, there was a fire in the neighborhood and we ran up toward the door of the place that had caught fire. Because that's your instinct—to just run in there and help. But it was so hot as we got close. To walk into something like that takes real courage.

While I was at the firehouse, posing for pictures in a firefighter hat and coat they let me wear, the alarm went off twice and the trucks moved out faster than I'd ever imagined. Crews headed to wherever the dispatcher had sent them, saved lives, then returned for pictures with me for the local media who'd come to cover the "event" of my being there.

Ironic, huh? I say "survey says" and get all this attention. But *these* are the people who deserve it. I found myself thinking about these guys' and gals' families— what they go through when the "event" being covered turns deadly. For someone holding a job like this, there's real impetus to not let issues remain hanging with your family.

Eventually, all excuses used up and distractions dealt with, I picked up the phone and called my oldest brother Frank. I prepared myself before I called. Being the oldest, Frank expects a certain reverence paid, and I know it's best to give it to him. *Let him be in control of this one, Louie.* I let Frank select where we—the Anderson clan—would meet. We decided to limit it to just the siblings and their spouses so there'd be some degree of intimacy. In the Twin Cities area, that comes to about a dozen Andersons.

Before the event itself, I headed over to Frank's house. Again, I was paying due respect. And actually, Frank and I got along pretty well. Maybe because we both like being in charge. Frank lives in a big house in one of these development communities where houses can easily go for half a million dollars. He and his wife Natalie live there with their cats—one of whom is the size of a pretty large dog. Frank, by the way, has given up his life of crime. In fact, he now gives lectures to companies about how to avoid getting ripped off by guys like him. Point to an object in Frank's house and he'll tell you how he *could* have stolen it—if he still did things like that. (In reality, he makes a nice living in a business that buys up mortgages from distressed hotels, then fixes up the hotels and resells them.)

Down in the basement, he keeps massive collections of stuff. Did you expect anything else from an Anderson? He collects replicas of old diners, lots of rare Indian artifacts he's come across, and a few prized Elvis dolls still in their original box. Frank is a pretty smart guy, having gone to college after he ran off to join the marines. He also gave I.Q. tests to people in prison for a while and learned a lot about human beings from that. I sat across from him as we talked about his Stickley furniture.

"You know, *they* were brothers who fought a lot," I pointed out.

"Oh yeah. Well, no wonder I have so much of their stuff."

We talked and laughed about our crazy family.

Then it was time to go to the restaurant. Frank had picked the Blue Fox Bar and Grill near the Target superstore, which is conveniently located near all the Andersons. I know some of the siblings wanted to have the event at their house, believing it would be more intimate. But that might have erupted in a turf war. This was fine with me.

The restaurant was nearly empty as we Andersons filed in: Sally, Sheryl, Tina, Kyle, Frank, and me—and the significant others, those who've been brave enough to hook into this family of ours. I had the waitress pull together the tables so we could sit together. In some cases, we hadn't seen each other in a couple of years. But it all started up again like it was yesterday. We hugged, talked, and ordered lots of food.

The waitress arrived with our breadsticks and my brother Kyle launched into a funny, crude routine regarding their phallic nature. We're old enough for the Viagra jokes, I guess. And Kyle is still the funny one in the family, although we all have our moments.

My sisters pulled out pictures of grandchildren, which went around the table. Proud grandparents. New hope for the future. Everyone was looking pretty good, considering.

When I'd walked in, I'd noticed that pull tabs were being sold at the front counter. They're like lotto tickets that you pull off. I went to the counter, bought a few hundred and put them in a basket for everyone to play. Maybe we'd come up with a few big winners. In the end, we didn't win much, but we Andersons like playing the game.

Kyle was the only one who brought presents. He handed me a box that contained a bright blue tie. I'd been trying to tone down my wardrobe, but how would he know that? See what I mean about presents? It *was* a thoughtful gesture, though. Kyle also brought with him some pictures from *The Oprah Winfrey Show*, which he handed to Sally and a couple others. I was glad to see the show had left no scars and was, in fact, a memory they seemed proud of. My siblings weren't nervous or shy on that show. They took it all in stride. True Andersons, ready for our moment.

My brother Frank got up to make a toast. He'd told me beforehand that he wanted to say something about Bill and Mary—the Andersons who weren't with us for the first time since we'd had one of these gatherings. "I know there are a lot of people who've had rough childhoods—you could probably find someone right here in this bar who's had it rougher than we had." Frank looked over toward the bar and then back. "Well . . . probably not."

We all laughed. It felt great, watching the whole family laugh like that.

Frank went on to talk about Bill and Mary. He spoke of how it was kind of hard to get to know Mary—like my sister Sally, she'd spent a lot of time with Uncle Ike and Aunt Iona, and so, for better and worse, had escaped some of our family's legacy. He then spoke about Bill, joking that he might know where Billy's gold is, but that if he found it, he wasn't going to split it.

There was more appreciative laughter. We all missed Billy. You could feel it. Maybe because deep down we knew that crazy was the only sane reaction to this family.

Frank asked me to say a few words. I didn't have much to say actually. I made a few jokes about Kyle's being a poster boy for emphysema. He was still smoking despite doctors' warnings. I told them that I, too, missed Bill and Mary, but that it was a pleasure to be here with the Andersons who were left. The survivors.

I handed out a bunch of tickets to the New Year's show. It's always hard to see family members when I'm performing, though, because I have to share myself not only with them but everyone else in the auditorium. The premise of my act is that we're all part of this one big kooky family. But *this* was what was real. Being with them now.

Heeding advice I offered in the early part of this book, I left at my appointed time—not the first to go, but not the last. We hugged and told each other how great it was to see each other again, that we really should be better about keeping in touch. I drove off, away from them, feeling . . .

I don't know *what* I felt at that moment. Holiday family gatherings—somehow you can't help thinking they should be like the ones depicted in those Christmas card photos. Or that Martha Stewart special. Come to think of it, Martha is pretty much alone in those shows. Oh, sometimes her mother visits, but who knows what really goes on. What was remarkable about my time with my family was how *un*remarkable it was. No hurt feelings. No dramas. No major incidents to report.

Partly, I guess I felt relief.

## FAMILY SURVIVAL TIPS
### (for holiday get-togethers)

**#47 Going to the movies.** While in Minneapolis, radio show host Ruth Kozlak told me that when she goes to family events she treats them as if she's in a play. Myself, I think of these events as movies I've seen before. The characters don't change, and the villain is still the villain. Uncle Harry is going to talk about your chrome-dome. Aunt Phyllis is going to ask if your wife is pregnant even though she knows she's not. My advice: Just relax and enjoy watching people play their parts. The only lines you can really change are your own.

**#48 Don't get wrapped up in gifts.** Realize that gifts can't change the relationship. Give the gift that you want to *yourself.* Then the other ones won't matter as much. Don't be afraid to tell people what you really want. And if all else fails, give cash. Seriously, if you really care about somebody and he cares about you, gifts don't matter. If the two of you aren't getting along, the gift itself won't fix much.

**#49 Lower your expectations (again).** Realize that no matter how much you eat, your mother's going to push food on you. And no matter how expensive a present you buy for your sister, she's going to think you're cheap. I have a friend who says he likes the "concept" of holidays. The concept is great. We just have to realize what's likely to happen when flawed people are asked to grab hold of an abstract thing like a concept and make it real.

# Family Hangover

**O**ften, after you've spent time with family, you have no idea how much it's affected you until someone points it out. During the photo shoot for this book, my hair and makeup person, Yvonne, was shaken up because she'd just had a car accident. She started to tell me how she'd just played host to her relatives for nine days. She loves her family very much, but nine days is a long time—family-visiting-wise. I thought back to how many times in the past I'd lashed out at the wrong person or done something stupid because I'd just spent time with my family and gotten thrown.

Each time you see your relatives, you're confronting your whole past. *Of course,* you're going to get thrown.

I have to say, though, that this most recent visit with my family had been a bit different. I couldn't quite put my finger on it until I was back in L.A. and not even thinking about it. What triggered the "epiphany" was a call I received from Frank. He told me he'd never seen me so relaxed, so calm, so happy. He said he'd spoken to Kyle who'd said the same thing—that I just seemed in a good place, a real grounded place. We talked for a while longer, made some jokes, then hung up.

There was some bad commercial on TV—for a

phone company or McDonald's or some mutual fund, I can't remember—but suddenly I started to cry. I fought back the tears and wondered what was going on. Then I realized what my biggest fear had been all along.

To explain, I have to go back to *The Godfather* and its sequels one more time. Think about the final frames of each film. At the end of the first *Godfather*, Michael Corleone is alone. At the end of *Godfather Part II*, he's alone again. And in the third *Godfather*, he dies alone in a garden—not even with his grandchild there beside him, as his father (the original godfather) had.

Isn't that what we're all afraid of—dying alone? And yet for those few minutes when I'd connected on the phone with my brother Frank—but more important, with myself—I wasn't alone. I was once and for all what I'd been that evening with my family—the tenth of eleven children of Louie and Ora Anderson.

And it felt good.

# Forgiveness

**N**o matter how hard I try, no matter how much money I spend, no matter how much I *pray*, there's no way I can change, fix, or reinvent my family. And you know what? The great thing is, I no longer *need* to try.